THE GUIDE TO WOODWORKING *with* KIDS

Publisher: Matthew Teague
Editor: A.J. Hamler
Design: Lindsay Hess
Layout: Alicia Freile
Photography: Doug Stowe, Danielle Atkins, A.J. Hamler
Index: Jay Kreider

Blue Hills Press
P.O. Box 239
Whites Creek, TN 37189
ISBN: 978-1-951217-23-5
e-book ISBN: 978-1-951217-32-7
Library of Congress Control Number: 2020934694
Printed in China
10 9 8 7 6 5

THE GUIDE TO WOODWORKING *with* KIDS

CRAFT PROJECTS *to* DEVELOP *the* LIFELONG SKILLS *of* YOUNG MAKERS

— DOUG STOWE —

CREATOR OF THE *Wisdom of the Hands* EDUCATION PROGRAM

CONTENTS

INTRODUCTION

"THE HANDS ARE THE CUTTING EDGE OF THE MIND."
— JACOB BRONOWSKI

I started the **Wisdom of the Hands** program at the Clear Spring School in Eureka, Ark., in 2001. At that time, woodshops in schools all across the U.S. were being discontinued with the thought that as a "service economy" in an "information age," woodworking was no longer relevant to our children's education. Policy makers and educators alike insisted all students were to go to college, by golly! The trades were considered a dead end. Manufacturing was a no-growth industry. And the idea that woodshop was relevant and valuable to our children's futures or their lives was no longer held dear at any level of American education.

"How could that be?" I wondered. After working in my own small woodshop for more than 20 years, I knew that woodworking was indeed relevant to every aspect of human culture. In the woodshop I used math, reading, writing, science, history, engineering, and design. As the son of a kindergarten teacher, I had long been interested in various theories of education. I felt that woodworking could stand at the center of a multidisciplinary approach to education, and deserved to be tested in a new light.

Years ago I restored an antique Ford including all the mechanics, the remaking of top bows, bodywork, paint, and even sewing the upholstery. I had literally taken the car down to bare bones, and rebuilt it from the frame up. The man who had helped by providing shop space and guidance asked one day when I was home from college, "Why are you studying to be a lawyer, when your brains are in your hands?"

I had no good answer at the time. But the question lingered. In school I made a sharp turn from political science, and began the study of ceramics. I moved to Arkansas as a professional potter and then became a woodworker.

My friend's observation was never far from my thoughts. Through years of projects I became an observer of the relationship between my hands and my brain, and new questions formed. If my brains are in my hands, is that not true for others as well? If that is true, even for some students, why aren't hands at the center of education? Of course the brain is in the head and the hands are at the ends of the arms, but the brain and hands comprise a learning system where each is so integral to the efforts of the other that to view them as separate is illogical.

As a new teacher in 2001 at the Clear Spring School, with the task of exploring the role of woodworking in education, I began building a program for high school students based in part on those I'd seen in the past, but also attempting to build parallel links to the students' core classroom studies. It was a challenge. Parents, students, and teachers needed convincing of the value of woodworking.

Could woodworking truly enhance more "intellectual" pursuits? Staff members were reluctant to admit that woodworking could be more than a vocational program, and integration into the body of the curriculum would take time.

In the fall of that same year while on my way to a woodworking educator's conference on the East Coast, I stopped in at the world famous North Bennet Street School in Boston. There, I explained my concept of the importance of hands-on learning, that doing real things by hand created both character and intelligence. They directed me to a nearly forgotten educational philosophy that had been important in the history of their school, called "Educational Sloyd," and that inspired me to research deeply into the history of the manual arts movement. That research led me to write articles in woodworking magazines, and helped to awaken my interest in manual arts education and particularly in Educational Sloyd. For me, and my program at the Clear Spring School, it led to expanding the program from high school only to offer regular woodworking for all students in grades K – 12.

This book is, in part, about that journey, but it's also intended as a road map and help guide for others wanting to bring woodworking and other forms of hands-on learning back into American schools and homes.

In 2006 I launched a Wisdom of the Hands blog to share the evolving philosophy I've used in the Clear Spring School woodshop, and to share projects with readers from around the world.

Through the years, I've been asked countless times for a curriculum based on Wisdom of the Hands or some means through which others could start similar programs in their own schools. I have no set curriculum to offer. What I hope to do is to inspire confidence, and offer a philosophy and a strategy for building a program of your own.

This book is organized to be useful to the teacher, parent, or grandparent interested in helping children develop skills of hand and mind. It is based in large part upon the learning principles taught in Educational Sloyd, first developed in Scandinavia during the 19th century. Those principles include a basic, but incredibly important concept: *Start with the interests of the child*. I'll talk a bit more about Sloyd in "Applying the Theory of Educational Sloyd" in the next section.

That brings us back to the Wisdom of the Hands. We learn more deeply and to greater lasting effect when we learn hands-on. Students have a strong inclination to do real things that may be of service to their families and communities.

One remaining point is that woodworking is an absolutely delightful thing to do with kids. They love it, even at all ages. And there is no greater gift we can give ourselves than to be a part of a child's growth of skill, character, creativity, and intelligence.

Join me, please.

Doug Stowe

APPLYING THE THEORY OF EDUCATIONAL SLOYD

The principles of Educational Sloyd came originally from Adolph Diesterweg, an educator in 19th century Germany. They were useful to his friend, Friedrich Froebel, inventor of kindergarten and early childhood education. Froebel's kindergarten, in turn, provided the model for education throughout Finland. Uno Cygnaeus, founder of the Finnish Folk Schools, established Educational Sloyd as a way to extend kindergarten learning methods involving play and creativity, into the upper grades. Educational Sloyd was, in turn, refined as an educational system by Otto Salomon and his many students at Nääs in Sweden. It was there that adult students from around the world learned the secret of effective education, and it spread to the U.S. and many other countries in the 1880s.

LEARNING THROUGH PLAY

The word Sloyd (or *slöjd*) meant "skilled" or "handy," and while some manual-arts training was launched purely to promote the skills needed for developing industry, Sloyd was derived from Friedrich Froebel's strategy of learning through play. Its purpose was to develop skill and creative capacity in the child, integrate the child as a productive member of society, and lead the child into meaningful participation in family, community and nation.

In Sweden, Otto Salomon developed a school for teaching teachers to teach Sloyd, and his school was responsible for sharing the method throughout the world. In his book, *The Theory of Educational Sloyd*, written in the late 1800s and translated into English,

Adolph Diesterweg, 1790-1866

Friedrich Froebel, 1782-1852

Uno Cygnaeus, 1810-1888

The Child as Craftsman

David Henry Feldman, a specialist in the study of gifted and talented children wrote an award-winning 1977 essay "The Child as Craftsman." He suggested the necessity of woodworking and other forms of artistry in development for each child. Feldman notes that all children have innate inclinations to seek excellence in some field of endeavor through which they can set themselves apart from their peers and earn the pride and recognition that entails. Those opportunities, with the loss of woodworking and the arts in school, have become few and far between.

Woodworking has long been suggested as being for those children destined for employment in the trades and manufacturing, but not for those who go on to work toward a college degree. The truth, however, is that every child, regardless of their career destination, can benefit when their hands are productively employed in creating useful and beautiful work. Feldman noted that, "...the main purpose of education [should be] to provide conditions under which each child will identify and find satisfaction through a chosen field or fields of work."

That field of expression might be different for each child. Work might be in music, athletics, or any other form of craftsmanship, including painting, theater, woodworking, and other arts through which their unbridled interests in learning will inevitably be aroused.

Jed Zapadka, a five-year-old from Coventry, Conn., beams as he displays the stepstool he built with his grandfather.

My own experience teaching at the Clear Spring School tells me that all children love woodworking and the creative environment that the woodshop provides. In the woodshop, children are able to make useful beauty while learning about themselves. Where schools do not provide this kind of direct learning, parents and grandparents must step in to fill the gap.

Salomon outlined the basic principles of education, upon which my own teaching is based. These principles were first described by Diesterweg as:

1. Start with the interests of the child.
2. Move from the known to the unknown.
3. From the easy to the more difficult.
4. From the simple to the complex and
5. From the concrete to the abstract.

In addition, Salomon recognized the ineffectiveness of classroom teaching, and proposed that individualized instruction offered significant advantages. This was very controversial at the time, as it would be today.

I use these principles to guide instruction in the Clear Spring School woodshop. I also offer the suggestion that the same principles offer profound benefits in all subject areas, in all schools and at all levels of instruction from pre-K through college.

MAKING IT WORK

So what does it mean to, "Start with the interests of the child?" Right off the bat, children love to be introduced to new tools that allow them to manipulate their environments, and allow them to see their own ideas brought into tactile form. So, woodworking is an activity that quickly captures the interests of the child.

Then, it offers greater opportunity when it can be used to fulfill a special connection related to a child's interests outside the classroom. For example, when one of my students had a particular interest in trains (and as many of my students have since), making trains fully engaged their interests and captured their attention for significant growth.

The knife is a classic example of moving from the known to the unknown. By the time Swedish children reached school age they had already learned to use the knife safely and without cutting themselves. Basic whittling would be a thing they had already explored and so knife work provided the foundation for further tool use.

Then, by using the knife and offering the students projects that expanded upon their previously acquired whittling skills, students were prompted to go from the known to the unknown. After that, it was a logical step for them to go from the very easy, to the use of the same tool in a more difficult and challenging way.

It was relatively easy for a teacher to build upon what a student knew. As more tools are added to the process and more demanding projects are offered, the child's growth from the simple to the complex naturally takes place.

Vol. II. THE No. 6.
CHRISTIAN EDUCATOR
A SCHOOL AND HOME MAGAZINE
JUNE
50¢ PER YEAR
5¢ PER COPY
HERR OTTO SALOMON,
1898
REVIEW AND HERALD PUBLISHING COMPANY,
CHICAGO, ILL. BATTLE CREEK, MICH. ATLANTA, GA.

Otto Salomon (1849-1907) depicted on the cover of an 1898 issue of *The Christian Educator*.

While much of schooling at that time was overly abstract, much of it remains so to this day as students are confined to desks, looking at representation of things in books or on screens rather than in "real life." To move from the concrete to the abstract required the teacher to present models to spark the students' creative imagination and to provide targets for their development of skill, just as I do in the Clear Spring Woodshop today.

Salomon's proposal concerning the ineffectiveness of classroom instruction is one that still bears true. In the woodshop at the Clear Spring School, I begin a project by describing and demonstrating the process of building

Enhancing Ability Through Stimulation

The role (and the power) of the senses is to confirm the reality, relevance and importance of learning. The chart seen here is taken from the book *Growing Up Gifted*, by Barbara Clark (Pearson, 2013). It illustrates the effects of environmental stimulation and how it strengthens the brain at the cellular level. A stronger brain, in turn, enhances a child's ability to learn and create.

It's clear when a child is not only learning, but also having fun while learning.

Recent research tells us that the children from rich parents perform better in education. That should come as no surprise. Their lives are often more deeply infused with experiences that are designed by their parents to offer a sense of mastery over the world that surrounds them.

Education has traditionally had three purposes. One was to prepare the child for economic success. Another was to force the child into compliance with societal norms. The third was to prepare the child (and, later, the adult) to get along with others within communities; to grow as human beings in understanding of self. To focus on doing all three is a tall order, particularly if you've created a contrived system of learning virtually devoid of real, meaningful work.

Woodworking is a great way to bring the senses (all of them) into school. It develops skills that can become a source of both amusement and the foundation for economic employment. It helps the child to understand societal norms and the value of all that surrounds us, and it provides a collaborative framework in which we work together in learning about ourselves.

By making schooling artificial, it becomes trivial. By making it a means through which children may serve family and community through the crafting of useful beauty, it is by no means trivial or abstract.

Enhanced ability to learn and create

↑

More creative, insightful, and intuitive thinking
More advanced and complex patterns of thought
Increase in speed of thought processes

↑

More effective and efficient neural system
More integration of brain functions

↑

Increased number of glial cells
Increase in dendritic branching
Stronger neural cell body

↑

Appropriate environmental stimulation

something, but what I demonstrate will not become truly clear to my students without first taking time to give personal instruction to each child. That is a lesson from the woodshop that should be accepted and understood in all classes, and schools and at all levels and subject areas of instruction.

PART I

MATERIALS AND PREPARATION

I'll discuss specific materials and hardware with the individual projects later in the book, but I thought it a good idea to go over a few basics up front. As far as wood goes, woodworking with kids is best done with softwoods—it's lighter, easier to cut, inexpensive, and readily available. I get most of the wood for kids' use from either white pine 1x4s and 1x6s, or from 2x4 lumber from the spruce and fir families. Spruce and fir are common in the construction trades as utility grade 2x4s, and are thus readily available at most lumberyards and home centers. White pine, spruce, and fir have two particular qualities in common: They can be cut easily with a saw, and can be nailed without splitting provided some care is used in placing the nails.

MATERIALS

As a furniture craftsman I had done most of my work using hardwoods. I keep a small supply of various hardwoods to introduce to my older students for a variety of projects, ranging from hardwood cutting boards to small furniture, boxes and other things reflecting their personal interests.

It is also important to use wood as a means to introduce students to the diversity of our forests. So, while softwoods provide most of the materials used in the Clear Spring School woodshop, we use other woods that are available. I find that ¼ in. luan plywood is great to use as platforms upon which students build a variety of fanciful things. This can be cut into pieces 10 in. x 12 in., or to larger and smaller sizes as requested.

Other materials you'll want on hand are dowels in various sizes, nails in various sizes and lengths, and glue. The dowel size we use most is ¼ in. diameter, as these are perfect for axles in toy cars, and also for the stems of wooden tops. In addition to wood, have a supply of scraps of other materials on hand, including leather, to customize projects. String and twine are also useful.

My students enjoy adding color to their projects, so a supply of paint and markers will also be required.

PREP IS KEY

Teachers, parents, and grandparents will find some power tools useful in preparing for lessons and woodworking activities for kids, and the table saw is useful to me in preparing stock, particularly for box making where various widths and thicknesses of wood are needed.

For example, in making stock for the box project later in the book, I cut the bottom and lid to thickness using the table saw. Due to the width of the material required,

To create two thinner boards from a thicker one, first run it through the table saw on one side, cutting halfway through.

Flip the workpiece end-for-end, and make another full pass through the saw, completing the cut and splitting the board into two pieces.

Always use a push stick whenever hands will be near the blade.

this necessitates cutting halfway through on one side, then flipping the stock end-for-end and cutting the other side to split the piece. You can prepare other material for the sides of a box the same way by ripping that material into the thicknesses required. Use a push stick to keep the fingers a safe distance from the blade.

Other tools useful for stock preparation include a compound miter saw to cut parts to length, particularly for box making with younger kids, and a bandsaw for preparing small parts. I also use the compound miter saw to cut long stock into shorter pieces before cutting them to thickness and width on the table saw.

PROCESS

Each tool, as it is introduced to the child, offers new possibilities and tends to excite the interests of the child. A curious, "How does that work?" is frequently followed by, "May I try?" So, the introduction of new tools on a gradual basis is a good way to sustain interest.

It is tempting to think that a shop full of tools is necessary for a woodworking program to be a success, but that's not the case. You can start with a simple inventory of tools, and gradually expand as it becomes clear that certain additional tools are required. In fact, this is a better approach than starting out with too large a burden of tools that must be mastered and integrated all at the same time.

The Principles of Educational Sloyd, described in the opening section, apply to the teacher's learning as well as to the child's. Start simple. A complex array of tools can come later. Start easy. Save some tools for later, after mastery of the basic ones makes mastery of the harder ones easier. Start with what you know and grow from there. This approach builds your teaching skills and your students' interests at the same time.

Einstein once said that his pencil and he were smarter than he was without it, and this can be said about every tool. Each is an instrument that increases human potential. Each is an embodiment of human experience and thought. Tools shape the way we see the world, and our places within it. They convey the potential of mastery, inviting us to think in new ways about the world and about ourselves. Tools can also be used mindlessly, or destructively, and to be entrusted with the use of a tool carries a responsibility. Shouldering the weight of responsible tool use is an opportunity that we must offer to all kids. It unleashes their potential to be smart, caring and responsible.

SHOP SAFETY

Woodworking offers inherent risks, which can be minimized or eliminated by the proper use of tools, and by employing a means to hold wood safely and securely as it is worked. A child may be injured by tool use, but a greater danger may be that a child never receives instruction in safe tool use, and uses tools anyway (as children will). Likewise, if made frightened and disinclined to use tools, a child will not receive the benefits of the creative power tools provide.

The first thing to know for keeping children safe in the woodshop has to do with understanding the way the hands work in parallel with each other. We have identified lefties and righties based on how they throw a pitch, or which hand they use to hold a pencil. The fact is that the hands generally work together in complete harmony. While one hand holds the pencil, the other steadies the paper as we write. While one hand may hold and pitch the ball, the other—and the arm attached—counterbalances and steadies the pitcher and is equally responsible for the ball's journey across the plate.

If you have doubts, try these things for yourself. Set a piece of paper on your desk and try to write on it using your "dominant" hand, but without holding it in place with the other. Or, try throwing a ball while your non-dominant hand is held tightly at your side. What you'll discover is that one hand works best with the collaboration of its mate.

This natural inclination to use both hands in a task poses a particular risk. The non-dominant hand is the one that is typically injured as tools slip.

HOLDING ON FOR SAFETY

One of the absolute keys in keeping children safe in the woodshop is training them in the use of the vise, clamps or other means of safely holding work as processes are performed on it. The vise is not to relieve the non-dominant hand from its work, but to keep it safe from being hammered, sawn or sliced with chisel or knife. It is also useful in most cases to have a third hand, which a vise or clamp provides.

At Clear Spring School, we have a room full of benches with vises sized for

A workbench vise will hold the stock as the student focuses on the proper use of the tool.

A handscrew and C-clamp can be used to hold stock in place of a bench vise.

both child and adult use. The vises are objects of fascination for kids, and they like to fiddle with them and squish things in them. Every classroom should be equipped with a workbench with a vise or two, and at one time many elementary school classrooms were so equipped with the recognition that kids need to be doing real things.

The point is not to discourage the use of the non-dominant hand, but that most tasks are actually better performed when *three* hands are available. This third hand may be that of a parent or teacher, and that's part of a lovely collaboration. But when students know how to use clamps and vises, they're better equipped to work safely and independently on things of their own design. This is particularly useful when there are several children in a class and the teacher cannot meet the demands of all children at the same time when they are asking for help. A good woodworking vise attaches underneath one end of a workbench and mounts flush with the worksurface.

Knowing that many parents and schools aren't able to get the right equipment in place, there are options. A bolt-down metalworking vise will work, even though it's likely to leave marks on the wood. Before I had a real woodworking vise of my own, and as a professional woodworker, I used wood-bodied handscrews to hold wood for safe sawing. The same can be true in the school woodshop. Use a large C-clamp to secure a conventional handscrew to the worksurface. For vigorous work, use two clamps to lock the handscrew in place. A good handscrew can be had for under $10.00, while clamps to hold the handscrew in place usually go for less than $5.00 each.

For regular woodworking without a vise, a simple device using a handscrew can be substituted. This is made with a piece of plywood to which the handscrew is affixed with screws. Because the

A more elaborate setup using a handscrew attached to a piece of plywood offers a firmer grip.

operation of a handscrew can be rather awkward for some to figure out, adult hands helping the child to secure wood in place may be useful at the start, while the student's hand strength develops along with understanding how the device operates. For more regular work the addition of a base to a handscrew makes it more convenient and easier to mount to a table or desk.

So what does a child do with two hands while the vise or handscrew functions as the third? I ask my smallest students to do one of two things, the first of which is to simply use both hands on the tool. Two hands are stronger than one and in many cases are called for. If that's not the case, I just have them put one hand behind their back.

With both hands on the saw, neither can be injured. The saw handle is large enough that both fit.

A hand behind the back is also a safe approach

EYES AND AGE

In addition to a vise or clamps or some other way to hold material being worked, there are two other safety concerns that are paramount. The first is that children should wear safety glasses in the shop, particularly when using tools or processes that generate dust or chips. Safety glasses are available in sizes to fit even the smallest child, and they are an inexpensive investment in child safety.

A second point has to do with the appropriate age at which various tools may be used.

Our students at the Clear Spring School are introduced to hand tools and their proper use at the first-grade level. They are allowed to use the drill press with supervision. I allow them to turn on the drill press and control the lever that lowers the drill into the wood while I hold the workpiece in place. The risk is that when the drill passes through the wood, that the workpiece may rise off the table and spin, endangering the hands. If I'm holding the workpiece securely to the table, that doesn't happen.

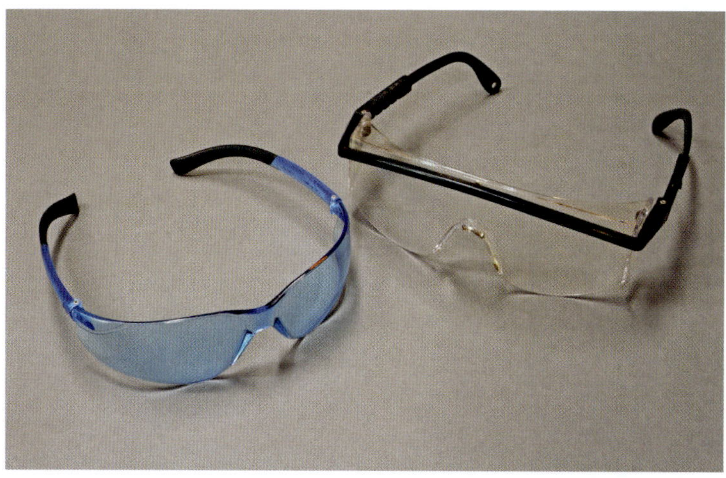

Safety glasses are readily available at low cost even for the smallest child.

They are allowed to use a battery-powered drill only when strong enough to hold it steadily, and if they have mounted the workpiece securely. The scrollsaw is available for their use only when they are tall enough and mature enough to guide the stock safely through the cut. That is generally when they are about in third grade. Up until then, I either offer to make the necessary cuts for them, or I recommend that they use a coping saw to make the curved cuts they have planned. By the time the students are ready to use the scrollsaw, they've watched multiple times how the saw is safely used.

We introduce the use of the lathe in the fourth grade, and reserve more dangerous tools for instructor use or closely supervised use in the upper grades.

TOOLS

"MAN IS A TOOL-USING ANIMAL. WITHOUT TOOLS HE IS NOTHING, WITH TOOLS HE IS ALL."
— THOMAS CARLYLE

I'll cover individual tools shortly in more depth, but first let's get an overview of the kinds of tools that work well for children. I frequently get requests for advice from teachers and school administrators about starting woodworking programs in their schools. I'm always experimenting to find better ways to teach, but I keep returning to the basic tools. A safe way to hold wood while it is cut is most important. As mentioned earlier, that can be wood-bodied handscrews mounted or clamped to a table or bench, or a more elaborate workbench with mounted vises.

You'll find that tools are a great way to spend money. You'll also find that knowing how they are to be used may become the first concern. Keeping things simple should be a basic philosophy. So, rather than go out and spend a lot of money on tools that may not fit your intent from the outset, build your program slowly and with clear intent. Not every woodworker or woodworking teacher will gravitate toward the same approach.

SAWS

In the way of saws I've used Japanese-style "Bear Saws" from Vaughan for many years that cut on the pull stroke, but have supplemented these with dovetail saws. The Bear Saws can either rip or crosscut.

You will also want some coping saws for curved cuts, and perhaps electric scrollsaws for grades three or four and up.

If you're using Western-style saws, as would a carpenter, consider adding sawhorses. These are handy when using your knee or body to hold the wood in place instead of in a vise.

I find a small bandsaw useful to make quick cuts in support of student work, along with a compound miter saw and table saw. These power tools are reserved for instructor use or closely supervised high school use only.

PLANES

I have a variety of planes, but primarily use block planes with the tote and knob kit that converts these to be better held in kids' hands and less likely to be dropped than would a standard block plane. The size and weight of these planes make them good for young hands, but without adversely affecting their use by older students.

SQUARES

I use shop-made wooden squares that are less likely to be damaged if dropped. Combination squares are prone to damage. (I've included a brief how-to in making a square coming up shortly.)

CHOPPING BLOCK

A chopping block is useful to have when students use chisels. This is simply a hard, sturdy piece of wood to use as a support base for chiseling, which keeps the work steady and protects the worksurface underneath.

SHARPENING TOOLS

I have a grinder for sharpening tools, but for planes you will need bench stones used with either water or oil, or some other means like sharpening paper and glass. While sharpening tools is a subject broader than the scope of this book, the ability to keep tools in proper tune is a regular and important task for a woodworking teacher. While Otto Salomon had suggested that trained teachers would make better woodworking teachers than to pull them from the ranks of accomplished craftsmen, the craftsman's love for and respect for tools is one area in which the tradesman might have a leg up over those who have training to teach, but no experience in woodworking.

RASPS

You may find rasps to be useful. Rasps and sanding blocks were not originally popular in Sloyd, as they can make the work less precise, but I've found them useful.

DRILL PRESS

We have two drill presses. One is a small bench model and the other a floor model.

KNIFE

We use Sloyd knives from Mora, Sweden, and I chose the short-bladed version of the knife to avoid the unnecessary length. We start the use of knives in first grade, but our groups are small and easy to supervise. Since this knife is so basic to Sloyd principles, let's begin the tool section with this versatile tool.

THE KNIFE

A blind man stands at the rear of an elephant and, while holding the tail, proclaims, "The elephant is a rope!" It is ironic that the simple Sloyd knife, one of "half a hundred tools" used in Sloyd training came to be its strongest symbol; the very slender tail of a complex educational system. In fact, the use of the knife was controversial even before the dawn of the 20th century.

S. Barter, in *Woodwork (The English Sloyd)* (Macmillan & Co., 1892), disparaged the knife in explaining the differences between the course of study in England and its Swedish origins. "One of the most important tools used in the Slöjd course, and certainly the most unique is the Slöjd knife. The advantages of this knife are not clearly brought out, though the importance of it is so strongly insisted upon; and moreover, it has been found that in this country that all work done with the knife can be more efficiently performed with a chisel. Under these circumstances, there seems to be no adequate reason for adopting an 'unfamiliar' knife in preference to a tool which is in such common use by all classes of workmen."

I had my own experiences with children and knives long before I learned about Sloyd. As a parent at the Clear Spring School, I went several times on the annual school campouts. To the surprise of many parents, children are encouraged to bring pocketknives (with locking blades) and are taught whittling. The teachers keep the knives until there is a safe time for the students to carve with instruction and careful supervision. These campouts continue to this day. It is a primal experience to sit at a campfire as boys and girls with freshly sharpened sticks heat-harden their points as our distant ancestors might have hardened their spears.

Sloyd Knives

These are two examples of Sloyd knives. One is an antique I brought back from Sweden in 2006, while the one in the foreground is currently made and of the type we use at the Clear Spring School. The short blade reduces risk and also requires less time and effort to sharpen. It is ideally suited to young hands. The availability of high quality Sloyd knives from Mora presented the first instance in which I heard the term Sloyd, meaning "skilled" or "handy." These were the traditional craft knives in Sweden that became known around the world in association with the international Sloyd movement.

According to Otto Salomon in *The Theory of Educational Sloyd*, "Every boy has many times, in a more or less elegant way, cut a stick with a knife, and is therefore more or less acquainted with the earliest exercises. We begin, then, with the instruments and exercises best known to the child, in order that our method of procedure may be as educational as possible."

Hans Thorbjörnsson, curator of Otto Salomon's library at Nääs, reminds us "Eighty percent of the Swedish people were living in the countryside about 1880, mostly farmers or farm workers and their families. Almost every farmer and worker wore a knife and probably used it daily. The boys took part in the farm-work from 8-10 years of age, going to school a few hours a day or each other day. Even these young boys used the knife in a natural way; they could handle it and were seldom injured."

Salomon found even greater purpose in the knife as reflected in the writings of one of his favorite authors whom he quoted frequently, the Norwegian Christian Jacobsen in his book *I Slöidsagen.Et Indlaeg* (Oslo, 1892).

"The knife demands total attention and permits no mechanical work. One can work start to finish with a single tool. Furthermore the knife can produce—unlike the plane as an example—curved surfaces in form work. This makes the knife superior when it comes to development of sense of form and beauty."

I recently found a Sloyd book for sale on the Internet. In the ad were the seller's words, "As if we could trust kids with tools, now."

And the great shame of it is we don't. Knives have become, for some children, objects of dark fantasies, dreadful weapons on the screens of computer games, fantasies played out in the news and then in the fears and worst nightmares of parents and school administrators. Ironically, the power to create and the power to destroy are both inherent in our relationship to our tools. We have choices whether they will be used to create form and beauty, or mayhem. Most schools are unlikely to introduce knives anytime soon, but even today's children need the opportunity to work with tools under the watchful eyes of parents, grandparents, and teachers, making things of beauty and purpose and discovering their own creative power. Just think of it! Children spending time in the woodshop!

In the very early days of Educational Sloyd training in Swedish schools, the knife was selected as the tool of first choice. There were several things about the knife that made it a perfect tool for beginning woodworkers. First, knives were commonplace and inexpensive. A small school could launch a program with very little expense. Many of the common woodworker's cutting tools like chisels and planes share the technology of steel and the knife's edge, so starting out with the knife gave students useful information that applied to other tools. In addition, the knife was a relatively complete tool, useful at all stages of a project from start to finish.

The knife is held in one hand, the piece of wood is held in the other, while a block of wood held in a vise or clamped to the table top serves as a third hand.

You could do projects with the knife alone, needing no other tools to finish the work.

All children at that time, particularly in the Scandinavian countries, were introduced to the use of the knife even before school age and were able to use a knife safely and effectively without cutting themselves. So the knife fit the educational philosophy of starting with the known and building from there. While some schools consider knives to be weapons and are concerned about children cutting themselves (or each other), that was never considered as a detriment to its use in Swedish schools. Knives offer an educational value that many other tools do not.

For instance, to use a knife in whittling requires close observation of wood grain and the character and various densities of the materials. You can start a saw in its cut and let your mind wander while your arm moves mechanically and the saw does its work. Not so with the knife. To observe closely and to modify one's response to what one observes, provides an introduction to problem-solving and the scientific method.

To make the use of a knife safer, practitioners of Educational Sloyd used a "three-handed approach." One hand held the workpiece and the other the knife, while a vise and a block of wood served as a third hand to brace the stock. This three-hand approach also centers the child's activity at a particular bench, removing the danger of students wandering around the shop carrying knives.

Training in the use of the knife can build a better understanding of the care that all tools require. Safe use of the knife does require some rules. The first is that children must stand at least an arm's length from each other. Particularly in the case of beginning woodworkers, all cuts should be directed

Out of doors the student is to hold the wood in one hand and cut away from the body with the knife. The seat of a wooden picnic table can also serve as a third hand.

An illustration from the original Sloyd teacher-training academy near Gothenburg, Sweden, shows a knife technique particularly appropriate for beginning craftsmen.

away from the body. In Sweden, and in the early days of Educational Sloyd in the U.S., students would mount a piece of wood in the vise to serve as a rest against which to prop the wood being carved, as is shown in the illustration from Nääs. Holding the wood in the vise allows the knife hand to exert greater force and have better control, while defining a carving space and boundaries for each student.

At the Clear Spring School, students are introduced to safe use of the knife at the first-grade level. They use them to sharpen sticks and to make writing pens they dip into ink to begin practice of cursive. All the students learn the safe and responsible use of the knife. Knives are kept where the students can pick one up, carefully adhere to the rules of knife safety, and continue to refine their technique.

Swedish Sloyd knives, racked and at the ready.

THE CLEAR SPRING SCHOOL WORKBENCH

Woodworking safely with children requires a bench vise to hold stock securely. While stools can raise a child to the height of your workbench, there is nothing safer than having your feet firmly planted on the ground for activities that require physical strength. While most woodworking tools are safe to the hands that hold them, injuries happen to hands left loose with their temptation to hold the wood or otherwise get in the way of sharp edges. A vise allows both hands to be used in holding the tool, or allows the other hand to be put safely behind the back. Either way, the hand most at risk is kept safe.

When we decided to introduce woodworking to elementary school students at the Clear Spring School, the first challenge was to make benches secure and stable enough to enable hand planing and rigorous sawing, that could be easily adjusted for students of different heights, and yet be light enough that they could be moved out of the way during middle- and high school classes. We also wanted benches that could be transported to the elementary school campus or other locations for special events.

Larry Williams, an expert in hand planes, helped me design and make these

Plywood "booties" fit over the bench legs to raise the height for larger children. A vise at each end allows the bench to accommodate two students at a time.

Blocking is necessary on the underside to thicken the wood for the vise to sit flush with the benchtop. Note the cutout in the end of the bench frame for the mechanism to move through it.

benches for Clear Spring. Based on the sawhorse concept, they have holes for bench dogs and 7 in. woodworking vises at each end. To make them adjustable for different working heights, without making the legs at all wobbly, we made "booties" to slip over the regular legs and act as extenders, adding 7¼ in. in height.

Blocks screwed on the underside of the benchtop hold the top in position within the structure of the bench.

One of my hopes in this design has been that it would be helpful to parents and grandparents interested in sharing their enjoyment of woodworking with their kids. This bench can grow with your child, and later serve as a heavy-duty supercharged sawhorse when your children are grown. We used vises at each end to allow 10 students at a time to work on our five benches. For a single grandchild, a single vise would suffice.

MAKING THE BENCH

We chose ½ in. Baltic birch plywood for structural panels with soft maple legs and tops. The soft maple had been a gift to the school from a forest products company, so while hard maple might have been preferred, in practice, the soft maple has offered sufficient resistance to wear—and it was free.

To attach the plywood to the legs, we used glue and an air-powered nail gun with 18-gauge brads. The combination of birch plywood, glue and solid maple provides a very rigid and stable structure, strong enough even for adult use. Additional stock must be glued and screwed to the underside of the top at the ends to bring the vise level with the surface of the benchtop. If making one of these benches, first buy the vise, as the opening at the end to allow for the mechanism to slide may be of different dimensions with different brands of vises.

Increase the capacity of the bench by adding extension blocks to the faces of the vise. These are simply bolted to the

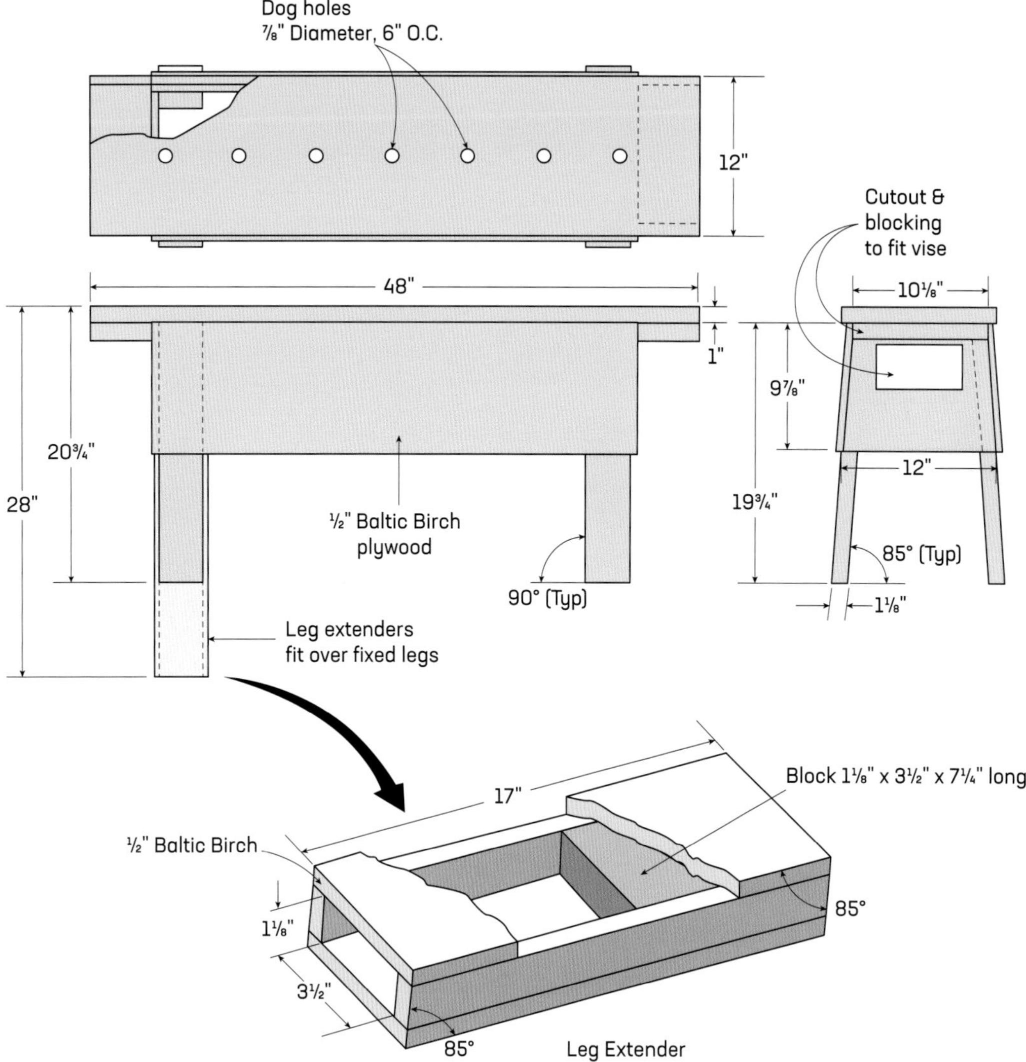

faces of the vise. In addition to making the vise wider, they also cushion the stock.

Another addition involves drilling dog holes in the top. These allow stock to be held between the adjustable dog built into the vise and a wooden dog placed in one of various holes positioned along the length of the benchtop.

Even when the workpiece is tilted for an angled cut, the vise holds it rock-solid.

A moveable wooden bench dog placed into holes along the benchtop works in concert with the vise's dog to secure long workpieces.

MAKE AND USE A SQUARE

Squares are tools with which students can evaluate and improve their work. Square ends on stock make the parts of a box fit. Square edges allow boards to nest tightly side by side for gluing or assembly. While some of my youngest students don't care if their cuts are square, an exercise in planing stock or squaring the ends of the stock invites the student to observe more closely the results of their efforts. In the process, it may help them to problem-solve or even anticipate problems before they are hatched.

In the Clear Spring School woodshop we use wood-bodied squares that I make myself. The advantage of a wood-bodied square is that it is lightweight, inexpensive and easy to replace. Unlike a metal square, it is unlikely to be damaged by the occasional fall from the workbench. The making of them is easy.

I plane stock to make the blade a thickness of ⅛ in., and then insert it into a saw kerf formed in the end of thicker stock. Provided the end of the stock is square and it passes in a vertical manner across the blade, the depth of the cut will be uniform and the blade of the square will automatically be "square."

Glue the blade of the square into the kerf. Before the glue dries, use a steel-bodied square (or any other object known to be perfectly square) to adjust the wooden blade to make certain it's square.

To use the square, the thicker leg is held tightly to the stock while you observe the relationship of the blade to the end or edge. To check an end cut, hold the square tightly to the side and end, and look for visible gaps. Hold it up to the light and if no light passes between the blade and the end of the stock, the end is square.

The two parts of a square are easy to make, and can be assembled and glued by your students for their own use and to take home in their toolboxes.

The same applies when checking the edge of planed stock. Look for gaps. If the body and blade both fit tight to the stock with no gaps, the edge of the stock is planed square.

One of the lessons from the square is that if you want to make a square cut, use a square when marking the line for the saw to follow. Box making in particular requires square cuts.

The finished square. You may drill a hole in the handle for hanging.

When in use, the body of the square is held tightly against the wood, and the blade is pulled tight to the end. Use this test with known-square stock to test your square. Any visible gap on one side of the blade or the other will indicate the blade is not yet in square. Check before the blade is permanently glued in place.

The square is useful when planing wood to make certain that the edge is kept square to the surface of the wood.

PLANES

Planes are among of my favorite tools in the woodshop. They are symbolic of an old way of doing things, and are very safe to use. While new ones can be expensive, you can find used ones at a reduced cost online or at flea markets if you're prepared to take some time to sharpen and tune them up. Regardless of whether you buy new or used, some sharpening skills are required and its best to take on that task yourself or assign it to older students, as it is easy to mess up a cutting edge.

When kids learn the correct methods from the start, they develop good habits. Good posture and the right grip lead to good planing.

We begin use of planes at the first-grade level. Students are pleased to see the curls of wood that form in the mouth of the plane, and with the smooth surface that results. Invite students to use their sense of touch and examine the freshly planed surfaces they get. The planes shown in the photo below include (front to back) a Veritas low-angle block plane, the same plane with a ball and tote option to make it easier for child use, and a 1950s Stanley Bailey #4 purchased used on the internet.

The general purpose of a plane is to make wood smooth and flat. But

Planes are both useful and interesting, as they create thin shavings of wood and leave smooth surfaces behind.

A shooting board used with a plane will square the ends of stock and can be used to bring two pieces to uniform length.

to do so requires attention to posture and technique. A plane can be used mindlessly with the results reflecting that. When introducing the use of the plane, introduce the use of the square at the same time so that the students have a means to evaluate and improve their work. Use a simple shop-made wooden square like the one found on page 30, or any good square available commercially. To check the work with a plane, hold the body of the square tight to the wood and see that the blade also fits tight with no apparent gaps showing.

Shooting boards provide a way that planes can be used to square up, and clean up a crosscut edge. A shooting board is among the simplest of fixtures, and consists of a square-edged board attached to a larger base. The workpiece to be planed rests against one edge of the smaller board, while the plane is used flat on its side. The arrangement holds everything in place while the plane slides at a right angle across the edges of the workpiece, squaring it.

SAWS

Some saws are designed to cut curves and some not. Some saws are good at cutting straight across the grain and others for ripping in-line with the grain. Here are a few that kids find easy to work with.

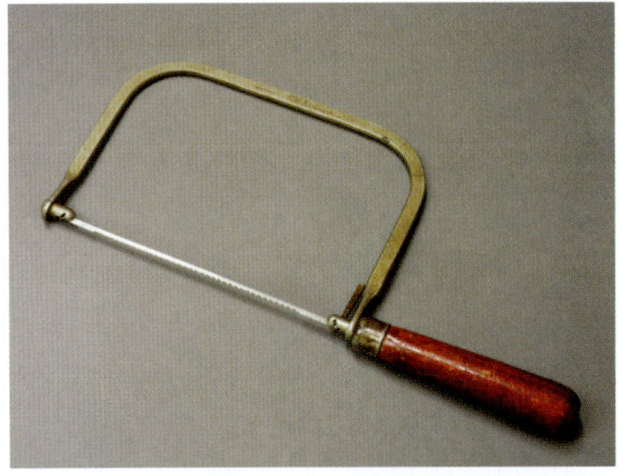

A common coping saw can cut circles, curves, and straight cuts.

TYPES OF SAWS

Carpenters use coping saws to "cope" joints in crown and base moldings. They can cut straight lines if you're particularly attentive and don't let your mind wander, but it's around curves that they that they find their best use.

The thin blade of the coping saw allows you to turn the blade during the cut, and the fine teeth are great for student use. Replacement blades are available from nearly any hardware store, so while the coping saw may not be well suited to heavy cutting, it might be the first saw you'd buy for student use. The blades are available in different widths, and with different tooth sizes. Fine teeth are the easiest to get started in the cut and cut more smoothly. Thin, narrow blades turn more easily, but are less suited to heavy work.

A dovetail saw—like the Veritas model shown in the lower photo on this page—cuts on the push stroke, and some young hands may find it hard to use. The challenge isn't in the saw, but in the user. With all saws, a smooth motion is required that, in turn, requires a smooth, consistent, and gentle motion of the arm. That can take some time and practice to master. It requires some attention to posture and body mechanics, which is a very good thing in itself. This is an excellent saw for a more skilled hand, particularly when using a miter box made to fit.

A dovetail saw is excellent for use with a miter box or for straight cuts.

The Vaughan "Bear Saw," like other Japanese-style saws, cuts on the pull-stroke, not the push. Its fine teeth are easy to get started in the cut, and the handle is large enough to provide for a two-handed grip. You will see each of these saws used in various projects at the Clear Spring School. We use the Bear Saw for angled cuts on thicker wood, and freehand cuts with the wood mounted in the vise.

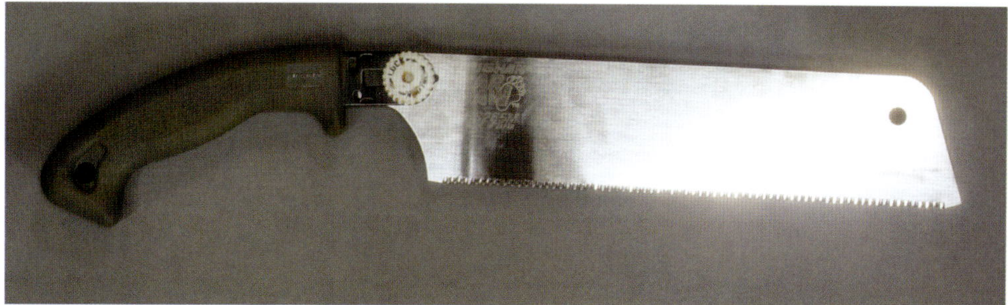

Japanese-style saws like this Vaughan "Bear Saw" cut on the pull stroke.

In addition to these saws, we also use a frame-style miter saw. This saw can be adjusted to a variety of angles and offers greater accuracy and longevity than a common miter box. Look for ones that have the ability to clamp stock in place during cutting. Large adult hands have a better ability to grip stock and hold it steady during the cut. Small child hands will benefit from clamps to hold material in place and allow both hands and the child's attention to be used to steady the saw's smooth motion through the cut.

Stanley's miter saw and miter box set feature a unique clamping system to secure the stock on both sides of the blade as it is cut. The clamping system consists of two plastic rods that fit into holes in the surface of the box and lock by twisting tightly against the workpiece. These are not useful for all lengths of stock—it's not possible to lock short pieces in place. A disadvantage of the Stanley miter box is that the plastic body doesn't allow for stop blocks to be clamped in place. The plastic is not firm

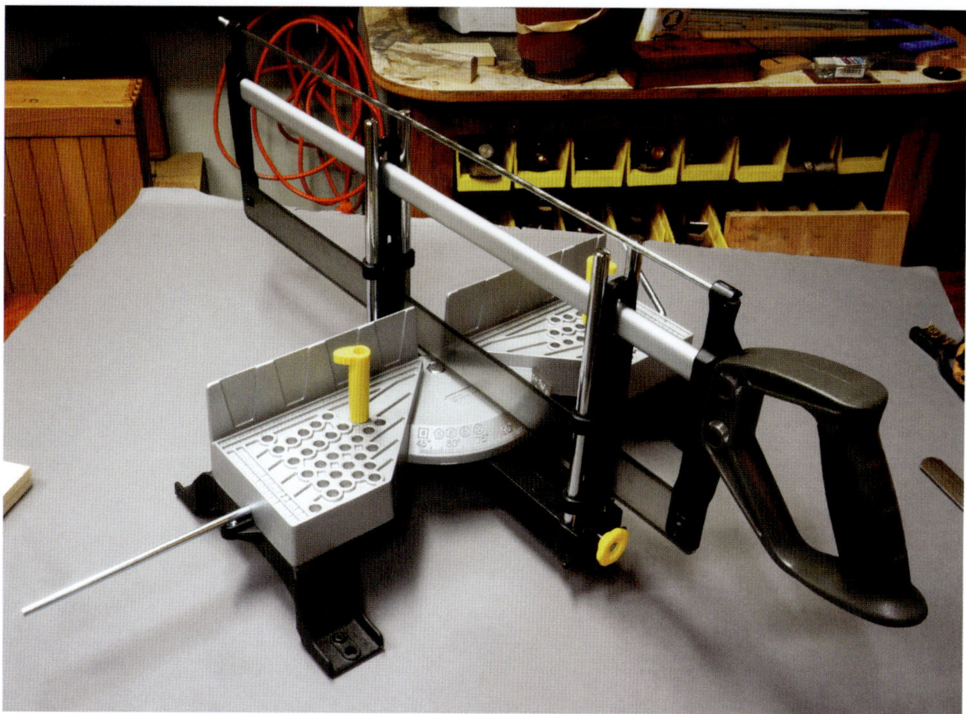

A frame style miter saw allows you to cut a wide range of various angles.

enough for that. Still, it's a decent basic miter box setup that is fairly inexpensive.

Miter boxes are particularly important when making something in which the parts must fit together precisely, as in making a box. Getting a square cut across the end of a board is a lot easier with the saw held at the precise 90-degree angle to the edge of the stock.

ADDITIONAL OPTIONS

There is always a tradeoff and arrival at a point of balance when it comes to choosing the right saw for the job. Do you want one that offers greater chance of success, or one that requires greater attention and development on the part of the child? Most often we are inclined to choose success over the risk of failure, but it's the risk of failure that offers the greatest chance for the development of skill.

We also have power saws in the Clear Spring School shop. The table saw is reserved for instructor use in preparing materials before classes. The compound miter saw is reserved for instructor use or high school use with careful one-on-one supervision. A bandsaw is reserved for instructor and high school use.

Scrollsaws are introduced for student use when they have sufficient strength and attention to safely control wood through the cut, which is usually by the end of third grade. By helping to guide their trial cuts at an earlier age, I can tell when they have developed sufficient strength of hand and understanding to go ahead on their own. It's like running alongside as a child rides a bike without training wheels for the first time. You can tell when they are ready for you to step back and allow them to go ahead on their own. Careful adjustment of the height of the guard appropriate to the thickness of the stock keeps the fingers from getting close to the blade.

A locking miter box and saw offer a quick way to get started, The saw works great and you can make a better miter box when the plastic one wears out from use.

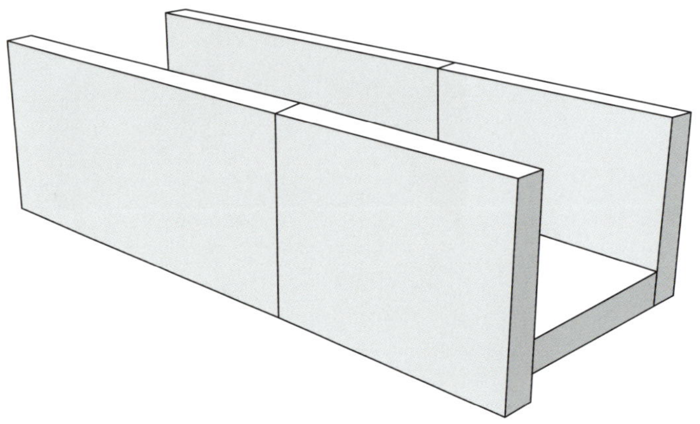

A simple shop made miter box is a perfect complement to any backsaw.

BORING AND DRILLING TOOLS

In the Clear Spring School woodshop we have two drill presses. One is a large floor-standing drill press that has greater power. The other is a small benchtop press that we use primarily for the students to make their own wheels. In addition, we have old-time crank-operated drills and battery-operated hand held portable drills.

The drill press generally gives the best results because its holes are always straight up and down regardless of student strength, steadiness, or posture. While I allow children as young as first grade to use the smaller drill press for making wheels, that's a special circumstance in which the wheel is held securely in a vise—if it was to come loose, it would spin without danger on the drill bit. In using the large drill press, because

Although Clear Spring School has a large floor-standing drill press, this smaller benchtop machine is easy to use anywhere in the shop.

Hand-crank drills are great for developing coordination, and safe in that both hands are required to grip the tool. Cordless drills are heavy, so look for smaller, lighter, less powerful drills for kids to use.

An adult hand holding the workpiece flat to the table of the drill press and against a wooden fence assure that the hole will be accurately placed and at no risk.

objects can be picked up by the spinning drill and knock knuckles, I insist that the young children in first though sixth grades not operate the drill without my assistance to hold the object being drilled flat to the table and against the fence.

In using hand-held drills, whether of the hand-crank style or cordless battery power, I demand they use a vise or system of clamps to hold the workpiece. The use of the vise is also helpful in avoiding drilling into the workbench.

HAMMERS AND NAILS

Probably the most common hammer in use is a 16 oz. carpentry hammer; however, those are too heavy for younger kids. The 10 oz. size (sometimes called a "ladies hammer") is a far better choice, and is also useful for high school kids or even adults. Most of our shop work at the Clear Spring School isn't carpentry that demands heavier blows, as would be the case in framing a house, so the smaller hammer is perfect.

A 10 oz. hammer and a common tack hammer.

Shop-made wooden mallets.

A good hammer will easily last a generation or more, so they are an investment that should be made early in a woodworking program. What you will look for in 10 oz. claw hammer is just for quality that will last. Tack hammers are also useful, but not as the primary hammer in the woodshop.

In addition to these hammers, we also use small wooden mallets that the students make using octagonal hardwood stock for the handles, and large wooden hardwood dowels for the hammerheads.

NAIL FACTS

Nails seem to be among the simple things we take for granted, and it may seem silly to write so much about them. But, while the use of nails in fine woodworking might be eschewed, in woodworking with kids using nails to attach pieces of wood to each other is essential. The first challenge is to know what nails to use and about the nail itself. This can take some careful observation. There are secrets to the nail that even many advanced carpenters have not taken the time to learn. One has to do with the point of the nail and using its orientation to avoid splitting wood.

Nails are easier to use in softwoods like white pine, spruce, or fir; harder woods like oak, cherry, walnut, and yellow pine tend to bend them before they are driven fully home. You will have some luck nailing some of the softer hardwoods.

How to Drive a Nail

There are some things to know about the use of a hammer in how to hit a nail:

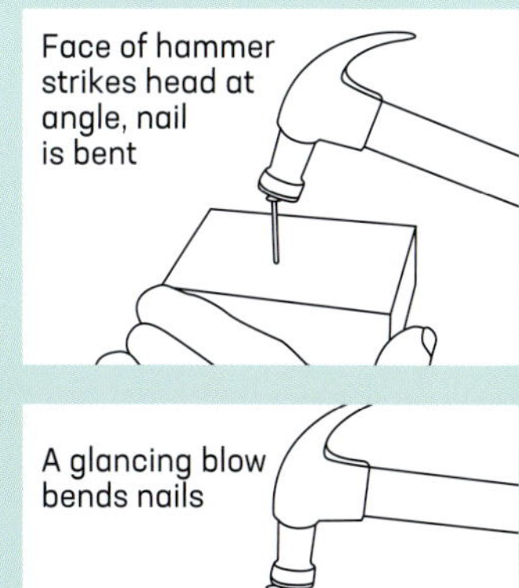

• If you hit the nail with the face of the hammer at an angle, it will bend the nail.

• If you hit a nail with the edge of the hammer face, it will bend the nail.

Hammer motion parallel to nail

Face of hammer square to nail

• To drive the nail straight, position the angle of the hammer and the face of the hammer to drive directly the center of the nail.

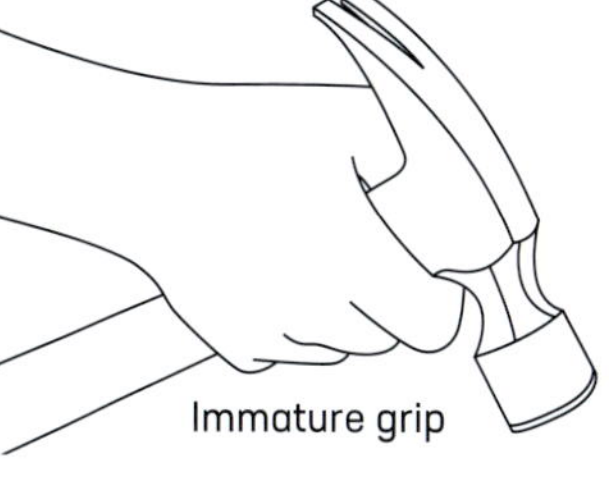

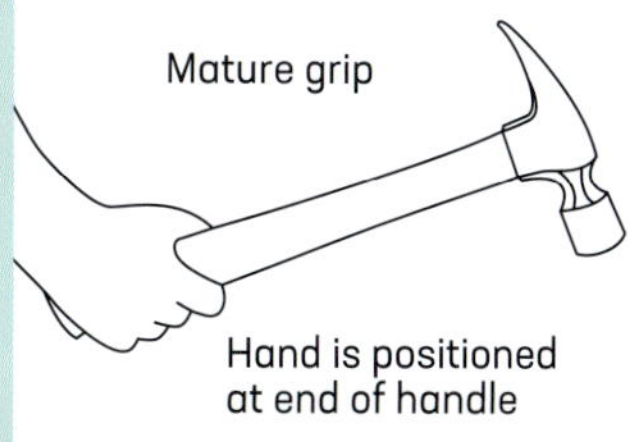

• It is most common for small children to hold the hammer up near the head. As they grow in strength of hand, comfort in the hammer's use and accuracy in directing the hammer's force, the hand will gradually recede to a more mature hand position.

While these aren't easy concepts to explain to a first grader, they're things they may learn through practice, particularly with your guidance.

For instance, basswood is soft enough under most circumstances to be successfully nailed. You can also nail the harder hardwoods, but you must drill pilot holes for the nails first, giving the nails a path to follow into the wood without splitting or bending.

In old houses, you'll sometimes find square forged nails holding together full-sized oak 2x4s. Those nails were driven into green wood in which the cells were still soft and pliant, allowing the nail to enter. Once the wood is dry, the nails are held fast. The wood actually shrinks tightly around the nail locking it in a tight grip. And you would never be able to pound those same nails into fully seasoned oak.

As a rule of thumb on selecting the right nail to fit the job, a nail should be long enough so that between half up to 2/3 of its length goes through the first board and into the one to which it is being attached. For example, to nail through 1/4 in. stock and into another piece of wood, the ideal length of nail would be 5/8 in. to 3/4 in. Nails longer than that tend to go astray, and shorter than that may give insufficient holding power. Of course the exception to this rule is when nailing two boards flat to each other, in which case the nail should be selected so that it does not go through both boards.

My youngest students like to just glue things together, but that tends to create fragile joints. Some students, on the other hand, love the challenge of nailing things together, even at odd angles, but often nails are made more effective if the wood is also glued. I sometimes have difficulty getting my students to do both. Effective nailing requires effective observation.

The drawing illustrates an important point in the anatomy of a nail. Anyone who has actually tried to hammer nails will have learned that they can either bend as they are driven or, if poorly placed, can split wood.

There is one little secret to nails that many of the finest carpenters may not know that can keep you or your students from splitting wood. To make use of this secret requires close observation of each nail as it is positioned to drive into the wood.

When nails are made, wire is pressed between two dies to form its head and point. The process leaves a small mark across the top of the head, and two sharp edges at points on opposite sides and parallel to the mark on the head. These sharp edges, when aligned at a 90-degree angle across the grain, cut into the grain and allow the nail to pierce the wood without splitting. If the nail is positioned so that these edges are parallel with the grain, the point of the nail works as a wedge, splitting the wood.

On very small nails like those used by kids in woodworking projects, the line at the top, and the tiny edges require close scrutiny. The edges are also sharp enough that you can determine proper orientation by feel. Learning the value of close observation is one more thing that students can learn in woodshop. This can be presented as a lesson on the value of close observation. Students can test the theory themselves to see if the lesson is true.

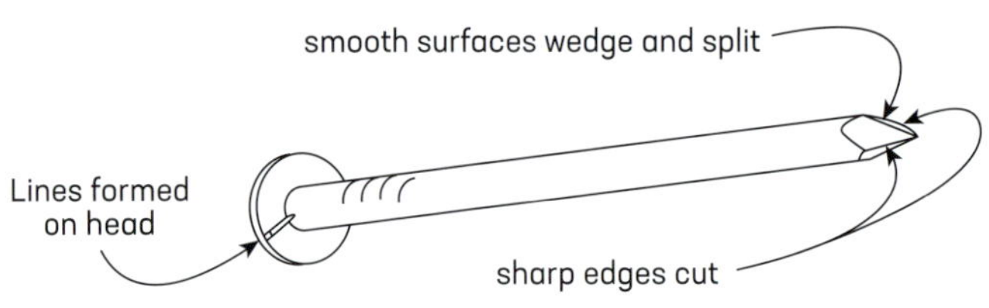

Align the sharp edges across the grain to avoid splitting. The sharp edges are formed by the dies used to shape the head and clip the point. A line parallel to the edges is formed on the head, top and bottom.

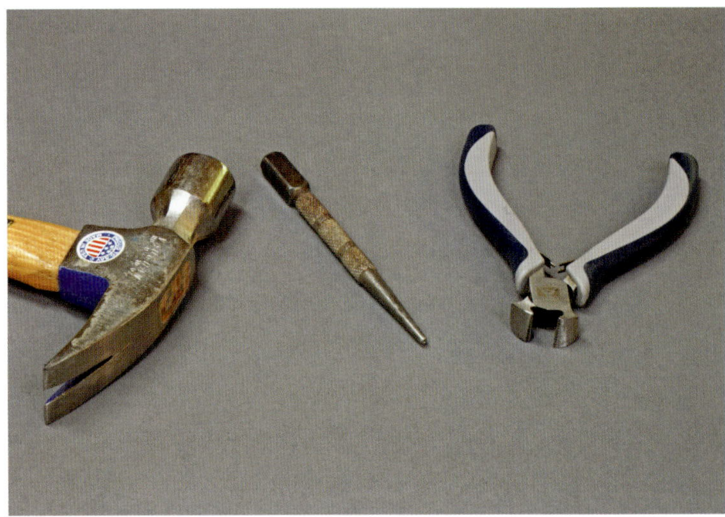

The necessities: a hammer, a nail set, and pliers for removing misdirected nails.

ADDITIONAL NAIL TOOLS

If your students are using nails, they will also need to know how to remove bent or wayward nails and to do so requires some extra tools. The claw end of a hammer is intended for nail removal, but works best on larger nails. The curve of the claw on the hammers we use is shallow, providing insufficient leverage. A thin block of wood between the hammer and worksurface increases effective leverage and cushions the material at the same time.

A small pair of pliers or end nippers is useful for getting a grip on small nails. Kids can be taught to use these themselves, alleviating the burden on the woodshop teacher, as bent nails are very common. Wayward nails like those that appear on the inside or outside of a box that are not noticed until after their heads are driven flush are hard to remove with either the claw or pliers. Use a nail set at the point of a nail to capture it and drive it out far enough so that the pliers can get a grip and pull it out.

Small nippers are perfect for pulling small nails. The students can be taught to do this themselves.

If the student has trouble pulling nails with the hammer claw, insert a thin block of wood under the head to increase leverage.

A nail set is useful not only for pushing nails below the surface of the wood, but also to push out nails that protrude in the wrong places.

THINGS TO WATCH FOR

There are two hazards associated with small nails. One is the problem of hitting fingers with the hammer as the nails are held trying to get them started in wood. With large nails, hitting the fingers or thumb can be avoided by using a simple strategy shown in the drawing. If the fingers holding the nail are toward the top, they are brushed aside by a hammer miss. Some professional carpenters will hold the nail between the fingers with the palm up, accomplishing the same effect.

The other issue is that small nails are frequently dropped and scattered, and the packages they come in are less than ideal for several children in the woodshop to share at the same time. I have simple tools to fix both problems.

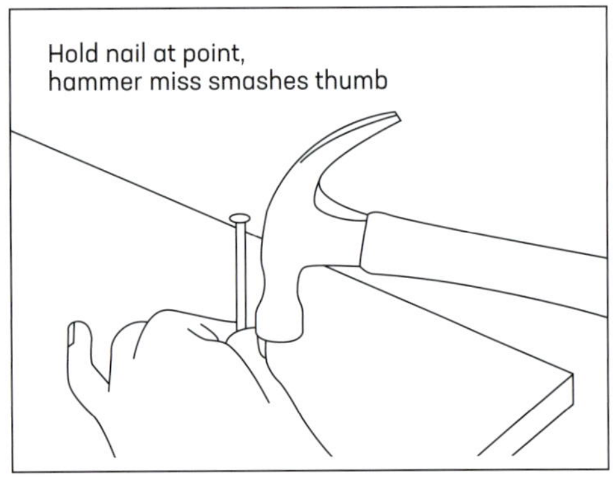

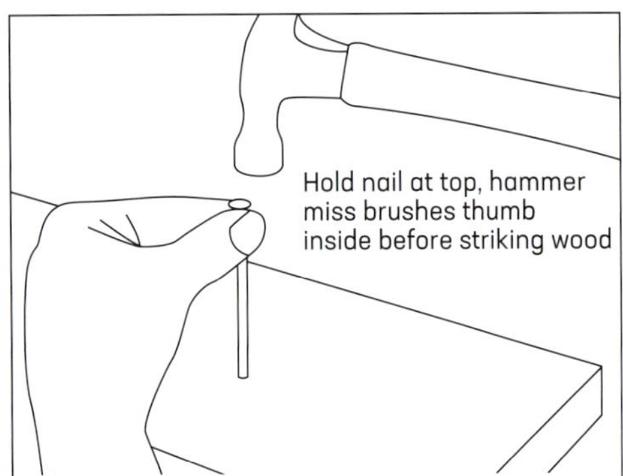

A simple thing: Where you hold the nail can help you to avoid injuries from misdirected hammer blows. This is especially important for teachers holding nails while the student drives them into the wood.

A simple tool for holding small nails while they are started in wood. This uses a rare earth magnet imbedded at the tip.

The first is a simple nail holder using a tiny rare earth magnet to hold the nail as it is hammered into place. It can be used by the child or by the adult attempting to help. To be able to nail with greater confidence is a big thing in the woodshop, making it a more pleasant experience for both adult and child.

Take a piece of hardwood, and plane or sand it to a thickness of ¼ in. and then drill a ⅛ in. hole for a ⅛ in. diameter rare earth magnet to fit. Glue that magnet in place using gel-type super glue. Shape the end to provide clearance for the hammer. As shown in the photo, you can use it on edge for larger nails, or flat to the wood for the tiniest brads.

The second problem solver is similar in that it holds nails and is made using a rare earth magnet. It's purpose is to hold nails outside of the packaging, and allow a box of small nails to be distributed

A magnet embedded into a piece of wood handily corrals loose nails

among students and then safely put away at the end of class without having to chase dropped nails all over the floor. Simply take a piece of ⅜ in. thick wood, cut it square and shape the edges (your preference). Drill a hole at the center to receive a rare earth magnet flush with the surface of the surrounding wood. It is easy to make one of these for each bench, and it will hold the nails of the right size for your project with fewer spilled nails and less waste.

SANDING AND SHAPING TOOLS

In the early days of Educational Sloyd, sanding was discouraged. Edges cut with a knife or plane were preferred, and sanding was thought to obliterate form. I can understand the point. Inaccurate tool use and inattention to grain can be hidden or disguised by sanding.

However, from the standpoint of a piece being useful and inviting to the touch, careful sanding is preferable to leaving rough edges unattended, and children like the tactile progression from rough to smooth. Additionally, using a knife requires constant attention to keep from injuring oneself, while the rasp and sanding stick do not.

Rasps are useful and safe in the school woodshop and provide a practical alternative to a knife. Put the workpiece in the vise to allow two-handed use of the tool. In the absence of rasps, sanding sticks serve a similar purpose. As a bonus, a sanding stick will remove coarse marks left by a rasp.

Sanding sticks and sanding blocks are easy to make in the woodshop at almost no cost. I make round sanding sticks by wrapping narrow sanding belt material around a dowel and tacking it into place. Simply choose a dowel, cut it to about a foot or slightly less in length and then tack a piece of sanding belt in place. Wrap the belt in a spiral around the dowel from one end to the other, and you have the perfect tool for smoothing an inside curve.

The rasp, knife, and sanding stick can work as a team to smooth and shape wood.

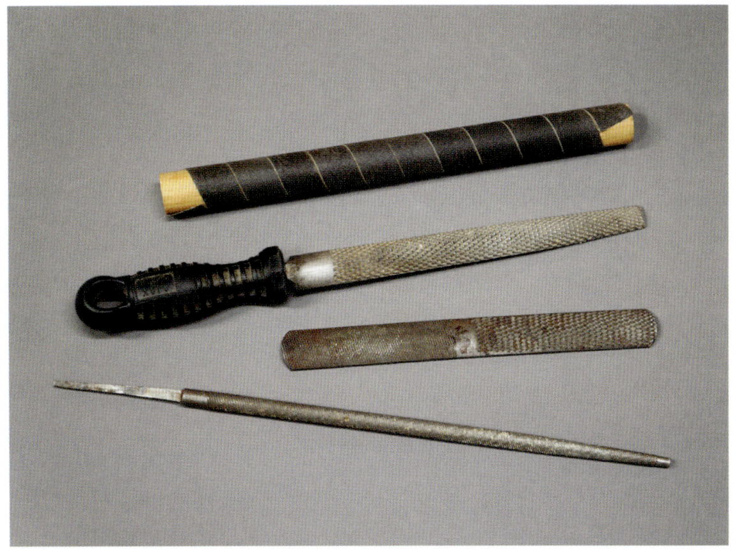

(From top) A dowel wrapped with sandpaper to make a sanding stick, coarse half-round file, 4-in-one shoe rasp, and a rat-tailed file.

For sanding flat surfaces or outside curves, use the same approach, but with the belt material tacked to each end of a flat block. I also use self-adhesive sandpaper to quickly make sanding blocks. Peel off the back layer, affix the sandpaper to the block, and cut away the corners to allow the ends to wrap without overlapping.

A third choice is to simply use self-adhesive sandpaper and stick it directly to the surface of a board or even a workbench. The problem with this approach is that the self-adhesive sandpaper can be hard to remove, but mineral spirits will dissolve the adhesive when needed.

For outside curves, we also use sanding belt material in thin strips. Put your workpiece in the vise and with a hand at each end of the belt, sand lightly by pulling the strip back and forth between your hands.

Shop-made sanding options include (from bottom) a sanding block made of self-adhesive sandpaper, sandpaper-wrapped dowel for inside curves, and a narrow strip of sanding belt that's pulled back and forth across the wood.

THE LATHE

The lathe, like the knife, is a nearly complete tool in that you can work from rough wood to a finished form using only a few other tools. No tool is better for the development of attention and mindfulness, or for an understanding of what it takes to develop quality. On the lathe, a student can begin with simple spindle turning and progress over a period of years toward hollow forms, bowls and other more challenging work. Younger students simply find it fascinating to watch as their direct action alters the shape of the wood.

As many adults have discovered, the lathe is a tool that offers many years of personal growth and creativity. Woodturners may practice for years and still discover new things around the next bend. You can start out turning simple spindles and candle sticks and progress over time to hollow formed vessels and bowls. This is true for kids, too, and can be a source of endless learning, fascination, and growth.

For fourth through eighth grade students, turning simple cylinders of wood and coloring them with markers can be safely done with experienced adult supervision. For high school students, turning bowls is a rewarding and challenging goal. We also turn wooden pens that the students use for calligraphy and practice writing.

There are values to be derived from the process well beyond the value of the object made. The lathe demands attention, and in a world of constant digital distraction, honing the ability to remain attentive pays dividends in every

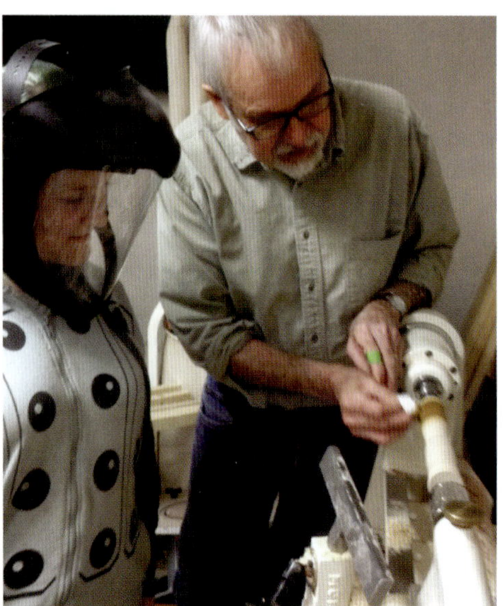

The lathe is a rewarding tool in a classroom setting, but close supervision and instruction are required.

Beauty in wood can be revealed and kept for generations.

Color can be added through the use of crayons and colored pencils.

possible career profession or recreational avocation. Further, to watch closely as the wood is transformed and as a stream of shavings flows from the tip of the tool, is deeply engaging.

SAFETY

Because the lathe can be dangerous, I only introduce it when students are tall enough and have shown sufficient maturity to use it as instructed. For safety, full-face masks are a required. No loose clothing and having long hair tied back are also rules that must be followed.

As a matter of course, I check each piece of wood mounted on the lathe to make certain it's secure. I also ensure that the tool rest is correctly set to provide proper clearance and leverage. I guide in the selection of the proper tools for the task, and make sure tools are sharp.

To teach use of the lathe requires the teacher to be well attuned to the practice of turning and attentive at all times,

Use full-face shields to assure safe work.

Proper grip of the tools is essential to keep fingers safe.

so I strongly recommend that teachers receive some lathe training in order to anticipate, and prevent, the kinds of dangers their students may face. An experienced woodturner can usually tell when something's not quite right by the sounds a lathe makes. So it's not difficult if you are listening to know when things are going wrong or right, or to anticipate when a student needs help.

The American Association of Woodturners is an international organization with local chapters that serve as a resource for anyone wanting to add woodturning to a school shop or to simply add to their own skills. Membership in the AAW offers a great way to develop an understanding of proper tool use and sharpening, and offers a means to stay abreast of the finest and most inspirational work. Woodturners tend to be friendly folks, quite willing to share what they've learned over years of experience. The organization has a strong commitment

Turning for kids

Woodturning can also be used as a way of making parts for furniture projects. For instance, a middle school class made this nine-legged bench with each student contributing a leg turned to their own design. Colored pencils were used to make the bench more colorful and an engraving in Viking rune proclaims the value of a good book. The bench occupies a special place in the Clear Spring School office where it is used daily by guests.

Students will compete with each other to achieve a surface quality that proclaims "smooth" to the touch.

Lathe-turned gavels and mallets add a challenge—and pride—as the students learn.

to the return of woodworking to schools. They often offer grants to schools to assist in the launch of woodturning programs.

FIRST STEPS

All students should begin by learning to turn a simple cylinder. They like to test and learn how each tool works and push the limits of the patterns they make, but simple shapes are much easier to create well. Complex patterns are difficult to sand and finish so I encourage simple, more elegant shapes whether turning candlesticks or bowls.

Some of the spindle projects our younger students make include candlesticks, tops, tool handles, mallets and gavels. Middle school students make their own turned pens and more complex objects, while our students begin bowl turning in high school.

An interesting thing that developed in lathe use at the Clear Spring School is that students have competed in achieving perfect or near-perfect smooth surface textures, offering compliments and encouragement to each other.

PART II

PREPARING FOR PROJECTS

One day, one of my first grade girls informed me that she wanted to make a skateboard. With no instruction or interference from me, she took four blocks of wood, attached wheels (I helped with the drilling) and she glued them to the bottom of a board. Was it a perfect skateboard? No way. But was it a valuable exercise?

Otto Salomon, one of founders of Educational Sloyd, once noted that the value of the carpenter's work is in the value of the object made, but that the value of the student's work, on the other hand, is in the student. It's certain that failure is a valuable instrument in education. A skateboard that breaks soon after being made from wooden wheels, dowels and chunks of 2x4 glued on a board may be of little value, but the value in the child having made it is priceless.

And that's the first thing to keep in mind as you enter this projects section. Most of these projects are very basic, but the real value lies in the experience you give a child.

HELPING KIDS LEARN

As with all the projects we do at the Clear Spring School, I begin preparation by making one myself. Having a finished example helps the teacher, parent, or grandparent know what materials are required, what challenges the child may face, and what safety concerns may arise. Then, there's the fact that if children see something they like, the impulse is to make one if the necessary tools, materials and know-how are at hand. Children are nearly always excited about woodworking and the opportunity to make something useful to them.

When making your prototypes, use tools similar to those your child will use so you'll anticipate the difficulties involved. I use a saw with fine teeth and secure workpieces in the vice just as they will. It helps to have a clear view of cut lines marked clearly in pencil, so I use a square to make certain lines are square. While many projects can be assembled with poorly cut lines, your job as teacher is to do your best work and set the best example. Younger children may not see the importance of the square, but no opportunity to demonstrate the way to achieve quality work is ever wasted.

Making toys is simply much more than making toys. There's a well-documented link between math skills and what is called spatial sense, described by the National Council of Teachers of Mathematics (NCTM) as "...an intuitive feel for one's surroundings and objects in them." According to the NCTM, "Geometry and spatial sense are fundamental components of mathematics education. They offer ways to interpret and reflect on our physical environment through abstraction. They support creative thought in all mathematics."

According to the standards, "...spatial visualization includes building and manipulating mental representations of shapes, relationships, and transformations."

All educators, whether in school or home, should focus on creating opportunities for the development of spatial sense. And making toys from wood is one direct means to cultivate spatial sense. Whether the toy is created by cutting away parts or by assembly of parts into a whole, the effect is the same. You'll do well to keep all of this in mind as you—and your kids—work through the projects to follow.

LUMBER SIZES

1x2	$^3/_4$" x $1^1/_2$"	2x2	$1^1/_2$" x $1^1/_2$"
1x3	$^3/_4$" x $2^1/_2$"	2x4	$1^1/_2$" x $3^1/_2$"
1x4	$^3/_4$" x $3^1/_2$"	2x6	$1^1/_2$" x $5^1/_2$"
1x6	$^3/_4$" x $5^1/_2$"	2x8	$1^1/_2$" x $7^1/_4$"
1x8	$^3/_4$" x $7^1/_4$"	2x10	$1^1/_2$" x $9^1/_4$"
1x10	$^3/_4$" x $9^1/_4$"	2x12	$1^1/_2$" x $11^1/_4$"
1x12	$^3/_4$" x $11^1/_4$"	4x4	$3^1/_2$" x $3^1/_2$"

A QUICK NOTE ON DIMENSIONS AND SIZES

Common lumber sizes go by a common nomenclature that, unfortunately, doesn't quite track with common reality. Since most of the wood you'll use will likely come from your local home center, you need to remember that actual dimensions of the wood found there are typically smaller than what the nominal size is. A project may call for, say, a 1x6 or 2x4, and that's exactly what you'll find in the racks at your local center. But the real dimensions of those boards are ¾ in. x 5½ in. and 1½ in. x 3½ in., respectively. Above is a handy chart that lists nominal lumber sizes and their true counterparts.

Speaking of size, although many of the projects list dimensions for components, you don't have to follow them religiously. These are simply the sizes that worked well for our students, so feel free to alter the dimensions based on design considerations, available stock—or any other reason at all. As long as all the components fit with one another in the finished projects, you can adjust and tweak dimensions to fit your material needs, and the whims and imagination of your young woodworkers.

PLATFORMS

Platforms can be … anything.

I keep a variety of pieces of scrap in small buckets in the Clear Spring School woodshop, and these are always available for students to explore and use in creative projects. If they finish an assigned project before the other students, these scraps help keep the kids interested for hours. We work best from the concrete to the abstract, and even a small, unusual piece of wood will sometimes stimulate ideas that lead to bigger things. As a practical matter, these scraps also serve as a ready supply from which small parts can be designed and cut to customize student work.

Towers and constructions of all kinds spring to life on a platform of thin plywood if sufficient scraps are kept on hand. Cubes of wood strengthen constructions.

A favorite activity in the lower grades is building on what we call "platforms" of variously sized rectangular pieces of plywood. And, since platforms serve as the foundations for a variety of woodworking projects, this seemed the most logical activity to use to kick off the projects section of this book.

The use of platforms started when I had some scrap plywood available and when students insisted that their favorite time in woodshop was when I would allow a "free day" in which they could work on projects of their own choosing.

A flat piece of wood can serve in wondrous ways. Platforms are often the starting point for a variety of building projects and function as experiments in engineering as students explore the limitations of gravity and glue in holding various parts and pieces in one piece.

Platform constructions are sometimes as simple as a kitty house (wooden, of course), complete with a toy cat and cat

Any flat piece of wood, large or small, becomes a "platform" with imaginative construction.

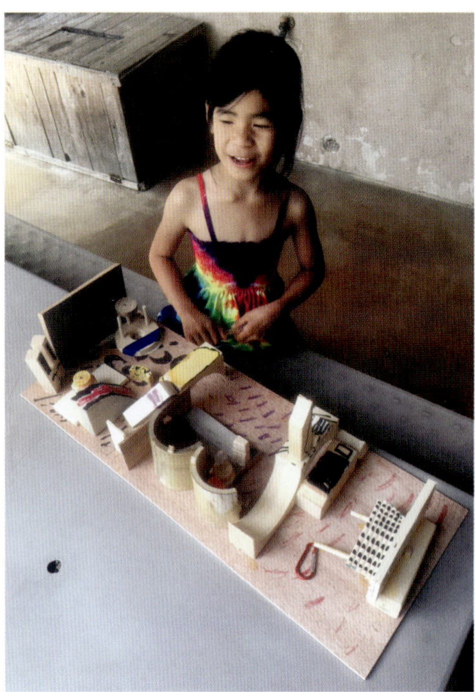

On a larger piece of wood, the whole range of intersection between childhood and the adult world can be explored.

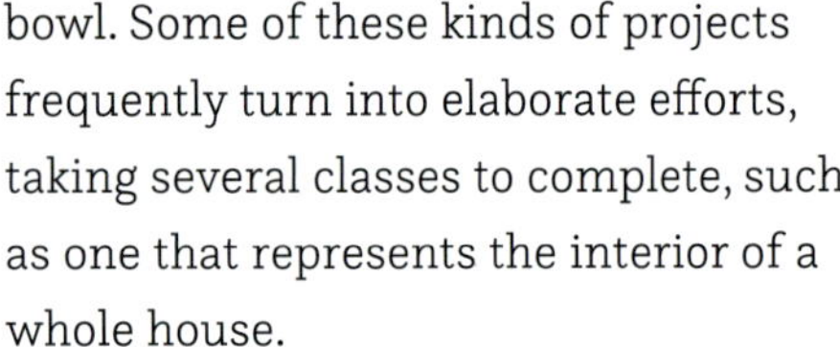

bowl. Some of these kinds of projects frequently turn into elaborate efforts, taking several classes to complete, such as one that represents the interior of a whole house.

Platforms also serve as an invitation to spontaneous collaboration, in which case the students share their ideas and build step-by-step together. These platforms become playgrounds for various toys they've made to use with them. Toy cats and robots are favorites. In addition to fundamental woodworking and design skills, the students also develop an understanding of very basic engineering, and hone their social skills through communication and collaboration.

Platforms present engineering challenges and require solutions that may not be readily apparent. For example, in order to get the trees to stand up on one platform project, the ends had to be shaped to fit holes drilled in blocks glued on top. Due to the complexity for their grade level, the tiny house shapes and triangular scraps were parts that my students requested my help with to complete this project.

"Will you cut this for me, please?" is something I hear a lot.

You probably will, too.

Collaborative platforms offer a perfect way to explore relationships.

Students bond and express collaborative creativity during the constructive play.

I get to help when the student says, "I need this, please."

A BASIC TOOLBOX

With your help, a custom toolbox for every child.

MATERIALS & TOOLS

- 1x6 white pine, 30 in. (actual size 3/4 in. x 5 1/2 in.)
- 1x4 white pine, 27 in. (actual size 3/4 in. x 3 1/2 in.)
- Nails, 1 1/2 in. and 2 in.
- Screws, 1 5/8 in.
- 7/8 in. dowel, 14 in.
- Plane
- Square
- Plane
- Clamps
- Vise
- Drill press with 7/8 in. and 5/16 in. bits
- Hammer
- Sanding block

You can make a simple toolbox for a child, but with a bit of your help kids can make their own. Best of all, by working together you can discuss what tools will be useful and how they might be organized, as once the box is made there are still opportunities to customize it to fit individual needs.

The toolbox is an important statement of trust, and suggests that children are to have tools of their own and are to be trusted to use them carefully and wisely. It also offers a place where they can be put away when not in use. With tools and knowledge of how to do things with them, our powers are amplified, and for children to understand their own creative capacity makes all the difference in the world.

Every woodworking project offers your children the opportunity to be creative. Allow your child or students to decorate and personalize their toolboxes with markers or paints and be prepared for the possibility that they will be useful for more than just tools.

2 Layout the toolbox ends. Use a tape measure and ruler to mark the shape of the toolbox end. When working with a classroom full of kids, I make this step easier by providing a marking template the exact size and shape as the ends. If working with just one or two children, take the time to instruct in the way to mark this out.

1 Cut the parts. Secure the wood in a vise to make your first cut and carefully guide the saw along the line. I keep a variety of saws on hand and this backsaw is more difficult for young hands to use than will be the Japanese pull saw I'll use a bit later. If your edge isn't perfectly square after being cut, use a shooting board and hand plane to square it up.

3 Clamp up for double-duty. To make things easier, use a clamp to hold the parts together as the cuts are made so they stay in alignment with each other. This way, you can cut both ends of the toolbox at the same time, and they'll be perfectly matched symmetrically. I used a Japanese-style pull saw to cut the angles in the toolbox ends, and found it helpful to align the cut line vertically so I didn't have to angle my wrists to make the cut—the cut follows the natural line offered by gravity. You'll need to rotate the stock in the vise and swap the clamp to the other side of the workpieces to make the angled cuts on both sides.

4 Refine the cuts. With the two end pieces still clamped, rotate them in the vise to a more horizontal position, and use a plane or sanding block to smooth the sawn edges.

5 Prepare for the handle. Hold the end pieces together as you drill for the handle to fit. I use a drill press and ⅞ in. drill bit to make handle holes through both ends at once. My students at the Clear Spring School love drilling holes using the drill press. They particularly want to do two things. The first is to control the on and off switch, and the second is to operate the handle that lowers the drill into the stock. This is one of those power tool operations that's safe for a child if an adult is attending. I ask that the child wear safety glasses, and that the drill press only be operated while I'm holding the material being drilled to the drill press table.

6 Prepare for assembly. Sand the edges of the toolbox before starting assembly. At this point, whether you are an adult or a child it makes sense to realize that you have only two hands and that they can only do two things at once if you want to do your best work. As you begin assembly, drive nails only part way in so that instead of holding the nail, holding the board in position, and hammering at the same time, you're only doing two things.

7 Setting the nails. Position your nails on the ends and drive them part way in. Be careful in placing your nails so they'll go through in the positions necessary to pass into the bottom board of the box. Once the nails are positioned and driven part way into the box ends, set them aside. Now, cut the box bottom to length and secure it in the vise.

8 Start with the ends. Apply glue to the mating areas to be nailed to give extra strength. Carefully align the first box end with the edges of the bottom and nail it into place. Then take the bottom out of the vise and align the other end and nail it into place. As you add the second end, be sure that the handle holes are in alignment.

9 Finishing up. Cut the sides to length and nail them into place. Now, slip the handle through the holes in the ends and glue it into place. I gently sanded the ends of the handle to make them softer to the touch.

10 Customize with some special touches. With the basic toolbox finished, you can take steps to customize it. Drill holes in the sides for pencils (a 5/16 in. bit works for most pencils). You can also add holders on the ends of the box sized for screwdrivers, scissors and all kinds of tools. First drill appropriate-sized holes in the holders, then glue and clamp them into place. When the glue has set, remove the clamps and drive screws into the holders from inside the box for lasting attachment.

MITER BOX

It's easy to make your own miter boxes for student use. This particular design will work with a wide range of saws, and can be adapted to most any saw: The height of the saw determines the height of the front and back pieces so the saw cuts only slightly into the surface of the miter box.

MATERIALS & TOOLS

- Base: ¾ x 4½ x 16 in. white pine
- Front left: ¾ x 4½ x 10 in. white pine
- Front right: ¾ x 4½ x 6 in. white pine
- Rear left: ¾ x 4 x 10 in. white pine
- Rear right: ¾ x 4 x 6 in. white pine
- 1½-in. #6 woodscrews, 10
- Glue
- Drill or screwdriver
- Square
- Masking tape

A simple miter box is one of the easiest ways to make square cuts with a handsaw. Unfortunately, today's mass-produced miter boxes have some deficiencies and it's best to make your own to ensure each cut is true. You can make your own miter box to fit the backsaw of your choice. Plan the height of the front and the back of the miter box so that the saw cuts only slightly into the base of the miter box. Making the components for this shop-made miter box requires the use of the table saw. While the completed miter box is for kids to use with handsaws, the construction of the box itself is an adult project. The miter box is designed to allow for a stop block to be clamped in place to control the length of parts and the front edge is deepened to rest against the front of a table or be clamped in a vise. Remember that in order for the miter box to be square and guide the saw to square cuts, special attention must be given at the start. Make sure the base of the miter box is cut square on the ends, and make certain that the rightmost pieces at the front and back are cut exactly equal in length and attached perfectly flush to the right-hand edge of the base.

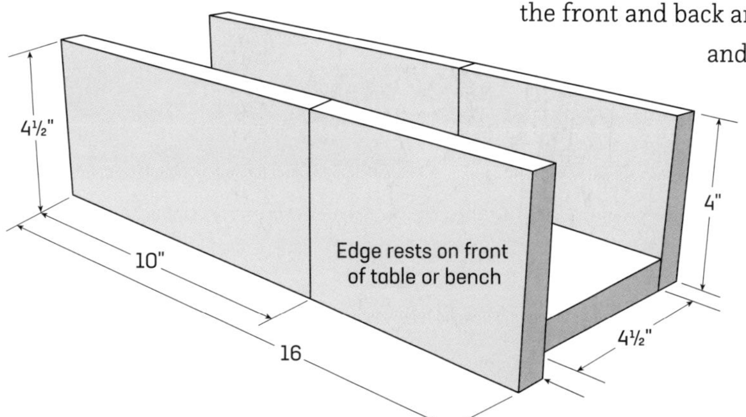

1 Use a screw to attach the first piece of the front fence to the base board. Note that I've positioned the board so that a portion of it extends below the base. This will either allow the miter box to be clamped in a vise or rest firmly against the edge of the workbench while you cut.

2 Use a square to make certain that the end of the front fence is square to the base before adding a second screw.

3 Use a square to align the back fence on the base. I have cut the back fence so that its height will equal the front, with the bottom edge flush with the underside of the base.

4 To make screwing on this piece easier, apply a bead of glue where the parts join. Tape the piece in position while the glue sets long enough (15 to 20 minutes) so that the piece will not move as screws are driven in.

5 **Finally, glue and tape the additional parts on the front and back of the miter box.** Leave a thin gap between the parts so that your saw blade will pass through. This will eliminate the need to make a full cut of your own and will increase the accuracy of each cut.

6 **Clamp a stop block to your miter box** to allow for consistent, uniform and repetitive cuts.

WHEELS, WHEELS, WHEELS

At the Clear Spring School, we make and use hundreds of wheels each year. They are used for everything a child can imagine from toy cars and trucks to student-made wooden skates and skateboards. The skates my students make aren't a huge success, but when a child is inclined to make something and test their engineering skills, I rarely stand in the way.

Every year we make toy cars and trucks at Christmas time to give to our local food bank for distribution to families. The students also like to make things for themselves and will choose one or more of the things they've made to keep or to give to family members. To give away something that you are proud of having made is a mark of growth.

Assorted ready-made wheels and axles can get you started.

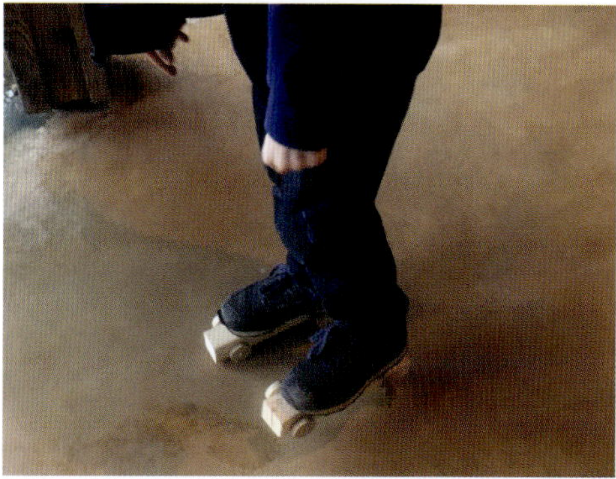

Even with projects that don't turn out well, like these wooden skates, there's still a valuable learning lesson.

In addition to wheels for toys, the same round disks of wood can be used for making tops and button toys, as in the short project boxes on pages 73 and 75.

You can purchase ready-made wheels by the hundreds at a reasonable cost. We bought the wheels shown in bulk from *www.caseyswood.com*, but most well-stocked craft stores also carry wheels in various sizes. These purchased wheels offer the advantage of being perfectly round, nicely finished, and are available in a variety of designs and sizes.

DOING IT OURSELVES

We make most of our own wheels. By using scrap dowels from a nearby handle factory that we get for free, the wheels we make have virtually no cost, and we're making good use of a by-product that might otherwise have gone to waste or been burned as fuel. Also, ready-made wheels and axles can cost more than a dime apiece and we don't want to be in the position of rationing their use. While we might run out of factory-made wheels, we will likely never run out of wheels we create ourselves.

By making wheels ourselves, the students have greater involvement and understanding of the entire process. They learn the use of the drill press, holding the wheels in the vise, or with a shop-made jig and are required to assist each other in the process. Our older kids can make more perfect wheels using the lathe, even from square lengths of wood, but that takes more expertise and greater maturity.

Few woodworkers will have the advantage of a nearby handle factory with scrap rounds of ash and hickory. Instead, make wheels from dowels, old broom and mop handles, or even from wooden closet rods available at your local lumberyard or home center.

In addition, you can make rustic wheels from tree branches. Simply cut a

Tree branches make a ready source for wheels. Although they won't be quite as round, they still complement a child's first woodworking project.

Bundle dowels with tape and use the bandsaw to cut wheel blanks. This works particularly well with smaller dowel sizes.

Use a table saw sled to cut disks of wood from dowels of various sizes. Closet rod stock from a home center and old broom handles may be useful.

section of limb and then proceed to cut disks from it with a handsaw. Often, the pith at the center of the disk provides an approximate center for drilling the axle hole. It's not entirely precise, but it's close enough to give the idea of a working car or truck. You can use a nail as the axle for these wheels.

Smaller wheels can be made using a bandsaw, in which case, you will want to bundle a group of smaller dowels with tape. This will keep individual dowels from twisting during the cut and jamming the bandsaw blade and, being bundled, keeps them from rolling off the saw table and onto the floor. You can also used a handsaw for this task, but to make as many wheels as we use at the Clear Spring School, the amount of labor involved would make buying wheels a more obvious choice.

For larger wheels, I begin by cutting disks from hardwood dowels using a crosscut sled on the table saw. If you opt to use a table saw, you'll need to clamp a stop block to the crosscut sled to assure uniform thickness of the wheels. I use a piece of wood as shown to hold the wheel in place throughout the cut. If not restrained, it can become trapped between the blade and the stop block and fly off in a dangerous manner. As you shorten the large dowel to the point you can no longer hold it safely with your fingers three inches or more from the blade, cease cutting and use what remains for other things.

KNOWING THE DRILL

There are several ways to drill the axle holes accurately at the centers. The techniques vary according to their accuracy and the time it takes to set up. The simplest technique is to use a jig geared specifically to the task.

Use a center-finding gauge to determine where to drill the hole, and then to use the drill press to do so.

A centering vise accurately positions the workpiece under the bit when drilling axle holes. Use a block of wood under the wheel to hold it at a more convenient height.

Another relatively simple way is to make a low fence with a V-shaped cut that allows wheel blanks of various sizes to nest in precise position under the drill. You'll find directions for making both of these handy aids in the next chapter, "Jigs for Making Wheels."

A drill press tool called a centering vise, typically used for drilling pen blanks for the lathe, will also hold wheels for accurate drilling. This is one of my preferred methods as it allows the students to safely drill the center holes themselves. Without the centering vise it's difficult for them to hold each wheel, as that may require adult strength to hold it in place and prevent it from spinning as it is drilled.

These holes may not be perfect, as the drill sometimes wanders as it follows the grain, but the success and learning offered by having made the wheels themselves is a benefit. I have the children work in pairs when they make wheels. One operates the drill press, turning it on and off, and lowering into the wood only when the other student has safely secured the wheel blank. Of course, the centering vise is also useful for making turned pens on the lathe, as we'll address in a later chapter.

You can also make wheels on the lathe, with their center holes drilled using a Jacobs chuck held in the tailstock,

Yet another way to drill axle holes in wheel disks is on the lathe. Hold the wheel disk in the chuck while the stationary drill in the Jacobs chuck is fed into the disk.

Tops

Tops are really easy for kids to make and decorate quickly. Then they love to play with them and give them to friends and family as gifts.

MATERIALS & TOOLS

- wooden wheels
- 1/4 in. dowel
- String
- Paint or markers
- Drill
- 1/4 in. drill bit
- Hand plane
- Vise
- Sander

INSTRUCTIONS

1 **Begin by drilling a 1/4 in.** hole at the center of a wheel disc. Then insert a stem with a sharpened end. To make top stems, tape 1/4 in. dowels together in a bundle to cut them to length for making several tops. To put tips on the dowels use an electric drill to spin the tips against a hand plane mounted in the vise, or against a belt sander, or disk sander.

2 **Decorate the tops with markers or paint and let the kids have fun with them.** The colorful tops become even more interesting when spun.

a ¼ in. drill bit, and some additional patience and skill. This is a task suitable for students who already have enough experience on the lathe to be trusted to use it safely. It offers the advantage of a well-centered axle hole, but use a brad point bit to get the best results.

Lastly, wheels must have axles. We make our own from ¼ in. dowel rods or ⅛ in. bamboo skewers. By taping a number of dowels together, you can cut them at the same time on the table saw, bandsaw, miter saw, or miter box.

Just as ready-made wooden wheels are available from suppliers, you can purchase axles for those wooden wheels at the same time.

Is the look of being ready-made an advantage or disadvantage in working with kids?

Whether cutting by hand with a miter box or on a bandsaw, taping dowels into a bundle makes the work safe and fast.

Factory-made wheels have the advantage of looking more professionally made. However, in addition to the cost of the wheels, consider the cost of ready-made axles if you choose to use them.

Button Toys

Button toys are quick toys and making them is a great way to help kids work on drilling carefully, without having to be too precise.

MATERIALS & TOOLS

- Wooden wheels
- String
- Paint or markers
- Drill
- 1/8 in. drill bit
- Vise
- Sander

INSTRUCTIONS

1 **Drill two 1/8 in.** holes on opposite sides of the center of a wooden disk while the disk is held safely in the vise. Then feed a string through the holes and tie the ends in a common square knot.

2 **Decorate button toys with markers or paint.** A small dowel is useful for applying paint. Simply dip one end of the dowel in a dab of paint, and apply it by dabbing the end of the dowel flat onto the wood.

3 **To operate the button toy, loop the string around the first fingers in each hand and gently swing it as shown.** As you pull the string tight and then relax and then pull again in rhythm, the disk will spin

JIGS FOR MAKING WHEELS

If you make a lot of wheels, here are two great jigs to make the task easier. The first is a small gauge that allows you to find and mark the exact center of a wheel (or other object). The other is a small auxiliary table that fits on your drill press that precisely lines up wheels for perfectly drilled holes right in the center.

MATERIALS & TOOLS

Center Finding Gauge:

- 1/8 in. plywood
- Saw
- Clamps
- Sandpaper

Wheel Drilling Jig:

- 1/2 in. plywood, sized slightly larger than drill press table
- 5/16 in. scrap hardwood
- Two 1/4 in. carriage bolts long enough to clear both jig and drill press table
- Two 1/4 in. Star knobs
- Router table with 5/16 in. straight bit
- Forstner bit sized to the head of the carriage bolts
- 1/8 in. and 1/4 in. drill bits
- Bandsaw
- Sandpaper
- Glue

INSTRUCTIONS - CENTER FINDER

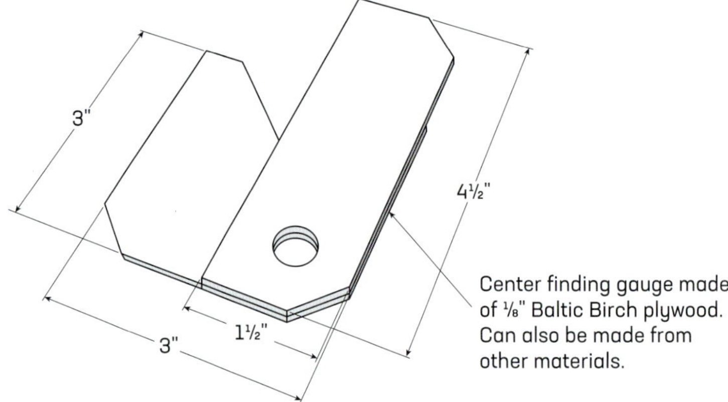

Center finding gauge made of ⅛" Baltic Birch plywood. Can also be made from other materials.

1 **Make intersecting 45-degree cuts.** Using the 45-degree angle sled on the table saw (a common tool for woodworkers) cut a "V" in a piece of ⅛ in. plywood for the base of the gauge, following the dimensions in the drawing for additional details. Use a stop block to position the cut, and then flip it about to cut the opposing angle to form the other side of the "V." As an option, you can use a handsaw, scrollsaw or bandsaw for this task, but may lose some accuracy in the finished gauge.

2 **Glue the upper portion to the base.** Cut the second part according to the dimensions in the drawing, and glue it to the first, making certain that the edges are aligned. Use clamps to hold the parts together as the glue sets. Double-check the alignment of parts before the glue dries, as the clamping pressure can cause the parts to shift. When the glue has set, you can give the gauge a light sanding and use it immediately, or do some additional shaping to better fit the hands. I drill holes in them so they can be hung up.

3 Using the gauge. Slide a wheel firmly into the "V" and use a sharp pencil to draw a line across the face of the wheel. Spin the wheel a few times and repeat with the pencil, and the center is found where the lines intersect. The test of their accuracy is when you draw lines in from the edge from several sides and have them intersect tightly on a single point as shown. You can also use the point of an awl or drill bit to make a small hole right at the center spot.

INSTRUCTIONS - DRILLING JIG

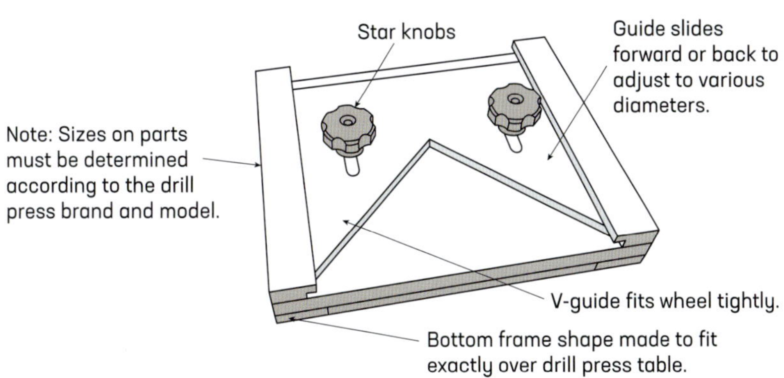

1 Prepare the underside of the jig. The bottom of this jig fits the exact dimensions of the drill press table so that it can be quickly positioned to drill wheel holes, or removed to allow the drill press to be used for other things. Use a piece of plywood large enough to more than cover the drill press table and then create a box form along the edges to exactly conform to the table dimensions. I used scrap walnut hardwood 5/16 in. thick and determined the width of the various parts by subtracting the size of the drill press table from the dimensions of the plywood and dividing by two. Use glue and clamps to attach the strips. Place the parts to allow for where the drill press table mounts to the column of the drill.

2 Attach guide strips to the top. Cut rabbeted guide pieces to control the position of the centering guide on the top of the jig. Flip the assembly over and glue these in place as shown, using clamps to hold it till dry. The rabbet along each piece should allow enough clearance for the centering guide to slide underneath as shown.

3 Rout guide slots. Use a router table to cut 5⁄16 in. slots in the centering guide for the bolts that will allow it to be clamped in position. Routing between stops allows the grooves in both sides to be exactly placed. The slots should be located so that they line up with the openings in your drill press table, allowing bolts to go all the way through.

4 **Drill the guide.** Mark the centerline of the jig carefully and position the guide and table so that a ⅛ in. drill bit chucked up in the drill press aligns perfectly with the centerline, and drill a hole. The distance from the front edge of the guide to the hole should equal one half the width of the guide. (If your guide is 10 in. wide, the hole should be 5 in. from the front edge.) This hole will be used for alignment every time the jig is mounted to the drill press.

5 Mark the guide notch. Use a combination square to mark lines from each of the front corners to the hole left by the drill. This will create a pair of 45-degree angles that intersect with the hole. Use a bandsaw or other means to cut on your lines, creating a "V"-shaped notch, and sand the edges smooth. This cut-away space will form the pocket for the wheel to fit as it is drilled.

6 Mark hole locations for adjustment knobs. The knobs can be loosened to allow the jig to be adapted to various diameters of wheel blank, and then tightened to hold everything in place. Set the guide up so the point of the notch is exactly beneath the drill bit, and mark the very back of the slots.

7 Drill bolt holes. Start by drilling a small pilot hole through each point, then flip the jig upside down and drill shallow holes at those locations just deep enough to house the heads of the ¼ in. carriage bolts that will be used from beneath the jig. Use a Forstner bit that matches the width of the carriage bolt heads. Now, drill bolt holes the rest of the way through from the upper side with a ¼ in. drill bit.

8 Use the knobs to adjust the jig. The jig should be set so the drill bit hits at the center of the wheel. The jig will need to be adjusted whenever you change wheel sizes. (Realignment with this centerline will also be required every time the jig is to be used.) An old fork with the ends of the tines bent at a 90-degree angle provides an excellent tool for holding small wheels in place as the axle holes are drilled. One student can control the fork, keeping both hands safe, while the other operates the drill.

VROOM

CARS, TRUCKS, AND OTHER VEHICLES

We make hundreds of toy cars and trucks each year at the Clear Spring School. Some of these are given to a local food bank for distribution to kids. Others are made as toys for our kids to keep and play with or to share with family members or friends. Most are built with wheels we make ourselves using inexpensive materials from our local lumberyard.

The students at Clear Spring School have made small mountains of toys to be given to children over the holidays. Each is different, and the children reap the reward of discovering their own creativity and generosity.

In addition to cars and trucks, we use the same techniques to make trains, planes, wagons, boats, and other things that come from the minds of our kids. The making of these toys, aside from their play value and the feelings of generosity they impart by donating them to worthy causes, is a valuable part of integrated activities and enhancing classroom studies. For example, in one lesson we made covered wagons and the horses to pull them. We then made the contents in scale model and the students wrote stories about their own imagined travels with their families along the Oregon Trail. In another lesson, we set up the making of toy trucks as an economics lesson, taking Henry Ford's production line and cost analysis and sales of the proceeds to cover the cost of a school trip.

Wheeled vehicles can offer a theme for integrated studies. In this case, wagons for an imaginary journey West are loaded up with supplies in scale sizes.

Just by changing the size and shape, a basic car becomes almost any kind of wheeled vehicle.

THE BASIC VEHICLE

Let's take a look at a typical example of a car, keeping in mind that the process is easily adapted for any vehicle. First make the car body in any shape you want. The one shown is ripped from 2x4 lumber at a thickness of 1 in., and then cut at a 30-degree angle at each end with a miter saw. You can make enough of these for a dozen kids or more in very little time.

Use a miter saw to make axles. Wrapping several dowels in tape allows you to make this cut without parts flying. Use a 5⁄16 in. drill bit to drill the axle holes completely through the car bodies from one side to the other. You will note that the axle holes are larger than the 1⁄4 in. dowels used for axles to allow easy rotation. I use a fence clamped to the drill press table so that the axle holes are uniformly placed the same distance from the bottom edge.

To prepare for car making, I'll have one small drill press set up to drill wheel holes (an operation students can safely perform in pairs) and the other drill press set up to drill axle holes through the bodies of their cars. (An operation for

When cutting axles with a miter saw, tape the dowels together for safety and efficiency.

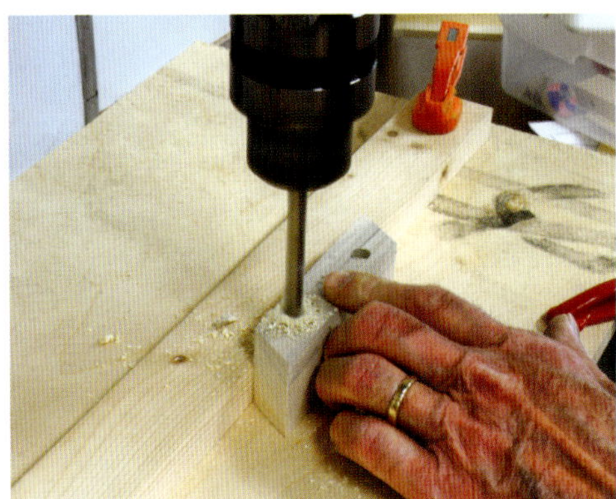

Use a fence on the drill press and a 5⁄16 in. diameter drill bit to drill axle holes in the body of the flip car.

To begin assembly, simply dip the axle dowels into a spot of glue and press each into one wheel.

With the axle through the hole in the body of the flip car, dip the end in glue to secure the other wheel. Be careful to not force the wheel on too tightly or it won't roll.

which I offer assistance by holding the body in place as the student drills). If the wood is not secured well during drilling, it may ride up and start spinning as the bit the goes through, putting knuckles at risk. The students like operating the drill press, but I insist being a part of the process to assure their safety.

Some of our toy vehicles start out as flip car bodies (see page 91) to which they've added parts to turn them into trucks, racers, or military vehicles. Some start out as larger 2x4 pieces 5 in. or 6 in. long. The students design cars directly in pencil on one side of the wood and then cut the shape out, or may ask me to do it for them.

Assembly is easy. Dip the end of a dowel in a spot of glue and insert it into the first wheel. If the fit is tight, use a small mallet or assembly hammer to tap it home. With the axle in the axle hole, and one wheel in place, dip the axle in the glue before adding the wheel on the opposite side.

With both wheels glued in place the student has a flip car to decorate, or a base from which to build other designs. A small tank complete with cannon barrel is an example.

The basic flip car easily converts to other vehicles like this tank.

ENDLESS OPTIONS

Blocks cut from 2x4 lumber can be cut to any size for making cars of various lengths and heights. Some of the cuts students make themselves using coping saws and the Japanese-style Bear Saw. When finished, the cars are thoroughly tested through play.

Fourth, fifth and sixth grade students are able to start their toy cars and trucks from scratch, using the scrollsaw to cut the car body to shape. With the exercise of student creativity, the cars often take the form of various animals such as a "cat car."

An important part of making cars is a session of play testing.

With wheels and colors, even a very simple block of wood can get into the act.

Even with the wood left unshaped, paint or markers can work wonders. The cars are ready for Christmas giving at our local food bank, and show that what starts out as a car may turn into something different in the mind of a child.

Trains are a favorite and have been made by multiple generations of first and second grade students at the Clear Spring School.

Wheeled vehicles can also be animals and pull toys.

Making Tiny Cars

Wooden dowels and 1/8 in. thick bamboo skewers offer a perfect combination of parts for making tiny cars.

MATERIALS & TOOLS

- Wooden car body of any shape
- 1/8 in. bamboo skewers
- Wooden wheels, drilled with 1/8 in. hole
- Glue
- Drill press with 1/8 in. and 3/8 in. drill bits
- Nippers or fine-cut saw

INSTRUCTIONS

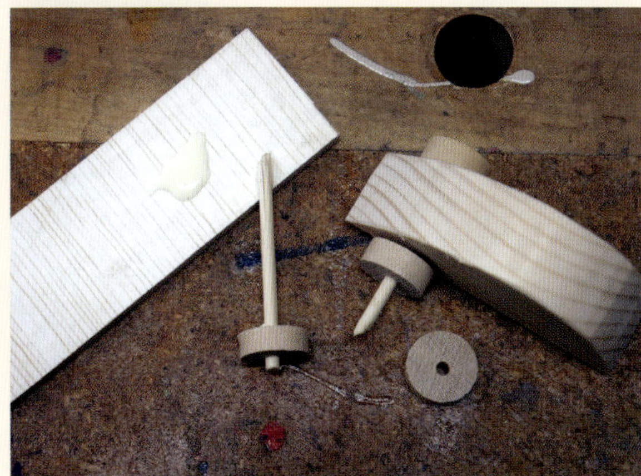

1 **Begin with any simple shape.** Drill 5/32 in. axle holes all the way through with a drill press. A small puddle of glue on a piece of scrap wood works great for dipping the ends of the axles before the wheels are put in place, thus assuring they will not come off. Don't push them on too tight against the body of the car or they will not turn.

2 **Trim axles.** Nippers are useful for trimming the axles flush with the surface of the wheels after the glue has set, or cut them off with a fine-cut saw.

3 **Make it your own.** Children like these from the Clear Spring School Kindergarten will not only want to make cars, they will want to customize them, adding pieces of scrap wood to turn them into other forms.

Kids can make cars of all kinds with a bit of wood, handsaw, wheels, and axles.

It is interesting how a single class with a group of kids can lead to such diverse results when their creativity is allowed and encouraged. The photo below shows a truck laden with stuff, a helicopter, a school bus and a tank surrounding a bed. A first-grade student made each of these items.

One last thing to keep in mind is that your assembly strategy may be a bit

Large-headed roofing nails can also be used as axles and simply driven into place through a hole in the wheel.

Flipping Fun

As a simple lesson making a toy car, I offer the flip car, one that not only rolls but changes from one model to another by pressing firmly on one end as shown in this series of photos. The slow school bus changes to a speedy racer in no time.

Making a simple flip car serves as an example of most of the toy cars we make. This car also serves as a platform upon which to build other car or truck shapes and body styles just by adding blocks of wood or scraps from other projects.

different if using ready-made wheels and axles. When using the assembly method discussed above, the wheels are glued into the ends of ¼ in. axles and the whole wheel/axle assembly turns in the body of the vehicle.

Ready-made axles fit into a smaller hole size and have heads that keep the wheel in place. Instead of gluing the wheels to the axles, the axles are glued into the car body and the wheels spin freely on the axles. You'll see this method used in the Toy Train project coming up in the next chapter.

TOY TRAINS

Toy trains are easy to make and an exciting task for children. In our small town we have a full-sized train ride excursion, so making an old-style steam train is a natural project to coordinate with a field trip and children's books on the subject.

MATERIALS & TOOLS

- 1½ in.-diameter dowel or wooden handrail stock, 3½ in. long (boiler)
- ¾ in. x 1½ in. x 6 in. long block of wood (carriage)
- 1½ in. x 1⅝ in. x 1⅝ in. (cab)
- 7/32 in. axle pins
- 6 wheels
- Use ¼ in. diameter dowels for smokestack and light, and your imagination for the rest
- Make additional train cars from solid blocks of wood, or assemble from parts as shown in the drawing
- Hooks and eyes, or fencing staples
- Saw
- Hand plane
- Vise
- Drill press with 7/32 in. bit
- Mallet
- Wire cutters or hacksaw

PATTERN

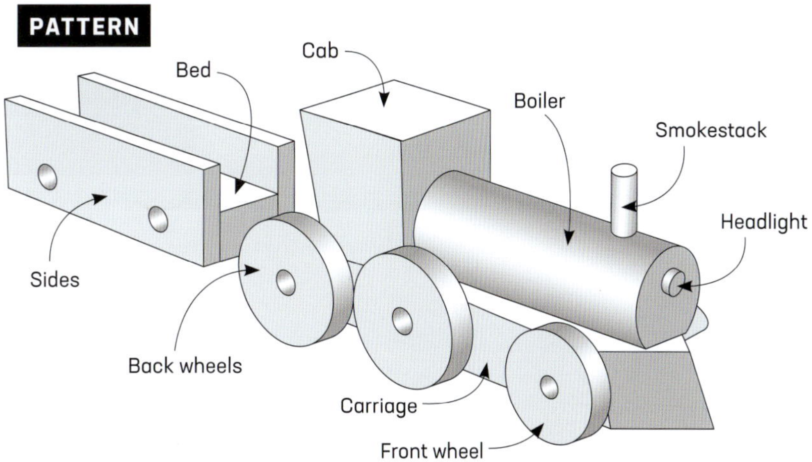

INSTRUCTIONS

1 Form a flat spot on the large dowel. Plane a flat spot on a 1½ in. dowel where it will fit onto the engine carriage block. An alternate approach might employ a piece of wooden handrail stock available in 8 ft. lengths from most local lumberyards. It will already have a flat spot along one side for mounting to the wall with handrail brackets. To use a hand plane, cut the dowel stock to length and mount it in the vise to plane as shown.

2 Drill for the axle pins to fit. Cut the carriage to come to a point at the front, and then use the drill press to make the axle holes. Use a thin spacer block to offset the distance from the bottom edge to compensate for the use of smaller wheels at the front. If using factory-made wheels, use a 7⁄32 in. drill bit for standard factory-made axle pins rather than dowels.

3 Glue in the axles. When ready to glue and hammer the axle pins into place, use a thin spacer as shown to keep the pins from going in too deep. There must be a modest amount of space to allow them to spin. Make a cab from 2x4 stock. Cut this at an angle at the back using a handsaw, and then glue it and the large dowel boiler into place.

4 **Create the connection points.** To connect one car to another as you add boxcars, flat cars, and the caboose, use small hooks and eyes from your local hardware store, or fencing staples as shown. Your child may need help with either approach. When using fencing staples, drive them in at a 90° angle to each other. Then use wire cutters or a hacksaw to cut one of the staples as shown, providing clearance for the two to interlock. Add axle pins or dowels to make a head light and stack as shown.

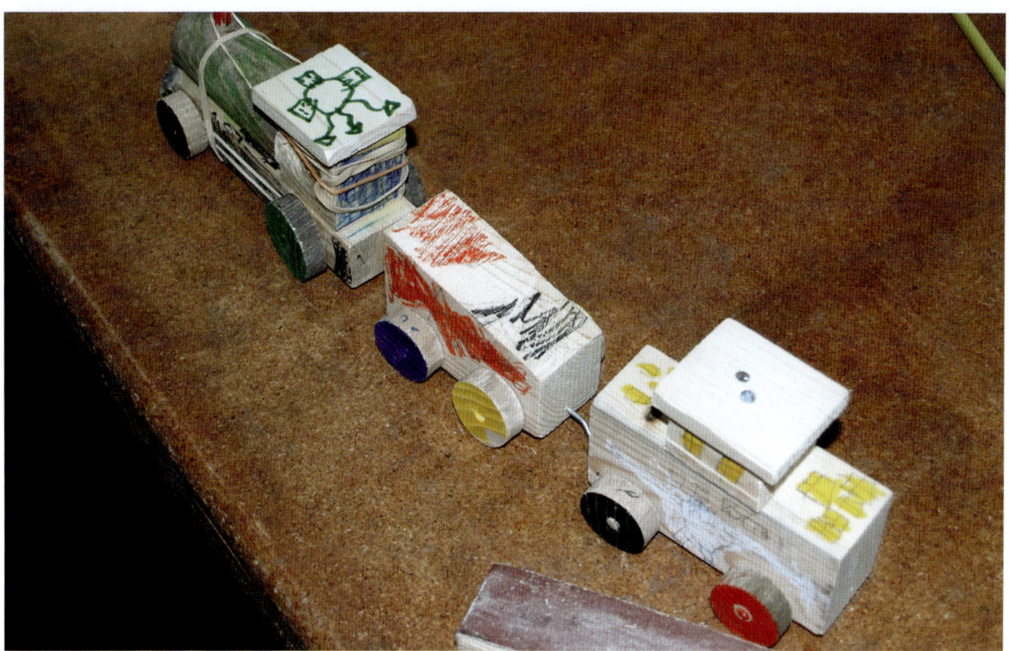

5 **Decorate and embellish.** When the train is complete, the child will enjoy decorating the train as desired! Paint, markers, crayons, and glitter are among the options for creative young minds.

L

SUPERHEROES, PUPPETS, AND ANIMALS

Characters of all kinds have been a mainstay in creative play for as long as you can imagine. When left to their own imaginations, you'll be stunned by the range of characters children come up with on their own.

We have made a variety of superheroes, puppets, dinosaurs and other animals over the years at the Clear Spring School, and these are particularly interesting for students in the lower grades. Fortunately, with children's imaginations at hand, these toys need not be too detailed. Much can be left to the imagination, while paints fill in details that cannot be made from wood. Dowels glued in holes suffice for legs and arms. A cape attached with glue or string turns a piece of wood into a superhero. A spike of stiff hair (yarn or twine) turns a block of wood into a troll doll, or the careful placement of nails at the top of the head transforms that same block into a robot. These are some of the simple tricks taught to me through the imagination of kids.

Dowels, a flat piece of wood, and a body made from a piece of 1x2 make a child's image of her dad as a surfer. Markers bring the work to life.

These toys are as appealing to boys as to girls, and are fantastic avenues for children to act out some of the ideas that are important to them. An example is the surfer shown at left that was made to represent the girl's dad, who is also a surfer.

Since the process for making these projects is similar, as are the results, it seemed a good idea to group them all together into a single chapter.

Superheroes

When our students began working on superheroes, they were encouraged to think of the superheroes in our own community. These were hospital workers, teachers, and even mom and dad. These weren't the fictional superheroes of the comics and movies, but real-life ones who live among us and are seldom recognized. As examples for my students to consider, I made two. One was a charcoal maker, filthy and terrifying in his day. My charcoal maker was inspired by a song and illustration from *Mother Play*, a collection of songs and illustrations created by Friedrich Froebel, inventor of kindergarten. Froebel's creation helped children understand the important role of the charcoal maker in their communities. The other was an obviously important librarian.

MATERIALS & TOOLS

- White pine or other softwood
- Glue
- Paint or markers
- Bandsaw
- Coping saw
- Vise
- Clamps
- Drill with ¼ in. drill bit and bit sized to twine or string

INSTRUCTIONS

1 **Prepare the stock.** Cut pieces of ¾ in. x 1½ in. white pine about 6 in. long. Using the fence on the bandsaw and a stop block to control the length of the cut, form the space between the legs. Using this simple technique, the parts for a number of students to make superheroes can be quickly done.

2 **Refine the legs.** Use a coping saw to cut away the waste wood between the legs. This is an easy process to demonstrate for your students, and relatively easy for them to do themselves. Cut in from one side and then from the other to remove the piece of wood. The stock must be safely held in a vise or secured to the worktable with clamps.

3 **Create the head and arms.** Cut the sides of the body to form the head and neck, then drill arm holes. Drill all the way to use a single dowel to create both arms, or drill both sides and use short pieces. With a handheld drill, secure the superhero in a vise. On a drill press, the child may do the drilling but the adult should hold the workpiece.

4 **Customize your creations.** My first grade students insisted some of their superheroes should be turned into cats, which they accomplished by adding small triangles of wood to create the cats' ears. Of course, a liberal use of colored markers helps complete the illusion.

5 **Wearing whiskers.** Whiskers, too, can be added by drilling into the sides of the head and gluing bits of twine into the holes. Some experimenting will be necessary to find the right size drill bit to fit the twine, which is simply doubled up and pushed in with a nail. When the glue sets, the whiskers are locked in place. Trust the child's creativity to kick into gear.

Puppets

A simple puppet design came about when our first and second grade teacher wanted her students to do a puppet performance of *The Hobbit*. Because the puppets needed some animation to their movements, I designed these with simple articulated arms and legs. The puppets are controlled by a dowel at the back.

MATERIALS & TOOLS

- White pine or other softwood
- Glue
- Paint or markers
- Construction wire
- Washers
- Nails
- ¼ in. dowel
- Square
- Coping saw
- Vise or clamps
- Pliers

INSTRUCTIONS

1 **Mark the leg cutouts.** Start with blocks of wood about 2 in. wide, 1¼ in. thick and 5 in. long. Use a square and pencil to mark the area for the legs to fit, and then mark lines from the end up to intersect with the previous lines.

2 Cut out the leg openings. I chose the coping saw to cut out the leg openings because of the ease with which the very fine teeth cut, but a Japanese-style pull saw or a dovetail saw would also work. Turn the stock onto each side to complete the cuts. You will note that the wood is safely held in the vise, and even an adult can demonstrate using both hands.

3 Cut the head. Rotate the workpiece in the vise and continue cutting with the coping saw to form the head. You or your kids can design the head as you like.

4 Make the arms and legs. Cut legs and arm to size, and drill holes all the way through the ends. I pair the two legs together and drill them so that the distance from the hole to the end on both will be exactly the same. Do the same thing with the arms. The holes will allow for a wire to pass through to connect the legs and serve as pilot holes to keep the arms from splitting as they are nailed into place.

5 Drill the puppet body. Using one leg as your guide, hold it in position on the body and drill a hole through for the wire that will connect the legs. Repeat for the arms.

6 Attach the legs. Make a small coil on one end of a wire (I use steel construction wire from the hardware store) and pass it through a washer, one leg, the body, through the other leg and a washer and form a coil on the other side. I simply grab one end of the wire with the pliers and twist. Use a hammer to flatten the assembly from both sides.

7 Attach the arms. To attach the arms, drive a nail in to hold one arm, then turn the body over to drive the opposite arm in place. Don't drive the nail in so far that the arms don't move freely.

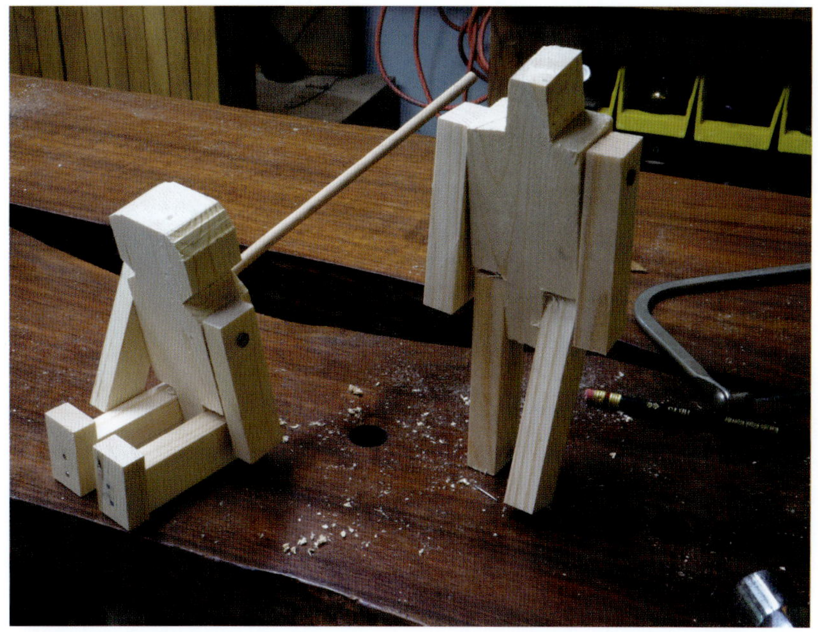

8 Add a control stick. Drill a ¼ in. hole in the back of the puppet, and glue in a length of ¼ in. dowel at the back to make a control stick for the puppet, or simply decorate and begin play.

9 Decorate and start playing. Allow your kids' imaginations to run wild with decorating their puppets any way they like with paint or markers.

10 Long-lasting fun. Don't be surprised if these puppets last a long time. This Captain America puppet received hours of play on the Clear Spring Playground. He was thrown down the slide, buried in sand, used as a target for slingshot practice and is still sound. He is a testament to the rugged and lasting nature of toys kids can make for themselves.

Horses and other animals

As I've already mentioned, young children have incredible imaginations, and are not dependent on extensive details to know what something is. For that reason, four dowels can serve as legs in making a horse.

MATERIALS & TOOLS

- White pine
- Dowels
- Glue
- Nails
- Twine
- Table saw
- Miter saw
- Handsaw
- Vise
- Plane
- Square
- Drill with ¼ in. drill bit and bit sized to twine

INSTRUCTIONS

1 **Prepare the workpieces.** To prepare the stock for student use, I planed 2x4 lumber down to 1⅜ in. thick, and then ripped it on the table saw to 3 in. wide. To make the parts easier to cut out, I made a template as shown here and used it to lay out the necessary cut lines, then used a miter saw to cut the parts to length at a 60-degree angle at each end.

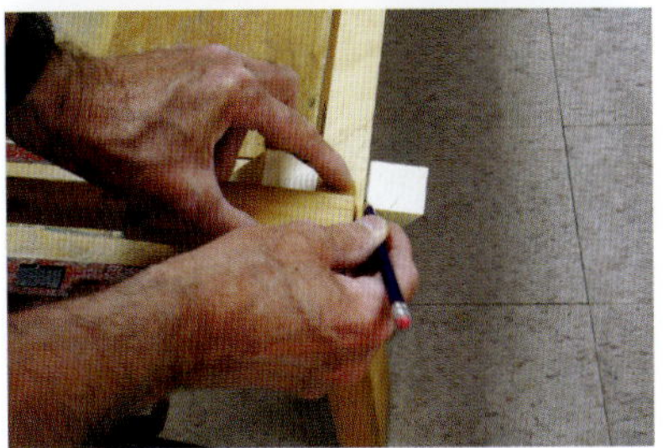

2 Mark for final cuts. Use the template and a square to mark the cutting lines on the workpiece.

3 An efficiency tip. To further refine the template, I cut it into two pieces so I could use it to mark the bodies of two separate horses from the single block of wood. If making teams of horses, each student can work with one block and cut it apart into two horses. If each student is making a single horse (or unicorn?) students can work in pairs and take turns making the cuts, each giving the other a chance to rest.

4 Cut the body. With the workpiece secured, begin cutting by putting the saw on the corner of the workpiece and pull, and then gradually lower the saw into the cut and along the lines you marked. To cut the block of wood into two bodies, re-orient the workpiece in the vise with the cut line vertical, and make the cut to separate the two pieces.

5 Drill holes for the legs. To drill dowel holes to a uniform depth, and to thereby get the horse to stand stable on its feet, tape the two horse bodies together and use the drill press with depth stop set to drill each hole to a uniform depth. Then hammer the dowels into place. If they are loose, use glue.

6 Create the heads. When forming the horses' heads, I use the bandsaw to prepare a number of them for student use in advance of the class. Students sometimes find pieces in the school scrap bin for use or design them for themselves. I first cut a block to the shape required, forming the nose and sides of the face first, and then make a cut across the top of the face forming the ears. It is then easy enough to cut that into three horse faces by making through cuts, dividing the previously formed block into individual parts.

7 Attach the head. Drill pilot holes to prevent splitting the wood and also to help you to position the nails used as eyes. Dab a bit of glue under the horse's head to give the attachment more strength, and then use a hammer to drive the nails into place while the body of the horse is held firmly with the vise.

8 Finishing touches. Drill holes in the head for the mane and at the end of the body for the tail. You may need to experiment with drill bit sizes depending on the size twine you use, but ⅛ in. is probably about right. Squeeze a bit of glue into each hole. And then twist bits of twine tight and stuff them into the holes. (Use a nail or toothpick to help push twine to the bottom of each hole.) The twine will not begin to look like a mane and tail until they've been untwisted, messed up and made wild.

9 Now, create a whole zoo. You can use this same technique to make just about any other animal as well. Play with shapes yourself first, and then design a strategy for you to demonstrate and for your students to follow.

PULL TOYS

Pull toys are a great exercise for older children to make and give to younger siblings or charitable causes. They're easy to cut and shape from a solid piece of wood, and with careful design you can cut two from a single piece of 2x4 stock. They are also easy to make, in that the holes required for axles to fit wheels need not be perfectly aligned. In fact, it's sometimes better if they aren't: If the wheels are slightly misaligned, the pull toy develops a "waddle" in its walk, adding a bit of real-life movement. Drill a hole for attaching a string, or use a steel fence staple and hammer it in place.

Using the imagination, two pull toys can be cut from a single block of wood. Two that I designed as models are a fish and a bird, both cut from a standard 2x4. Simply sketch the shapes on a piece of 2x4 stock and use a small bandsaw, scrollsaw or coping saw to divide the workpiece into two parts. Then drill axle holes, add wheels, and attach a pull string.

Others, like this simply made, wheeled creature at right, can be brought to life with the use of non-toxic acrylic paints or through the use of markers. Other options can make use of woods from the scrap bucket. Sketch directly on wood, cut the shape, and add wheels and string.

Student works may draw on previous experience making toy cars as in an earlier project chapter. This pull toy—a colorfully decorated little chick—is based upon the flip car chassis presented in the chapter "Cars, Trucks and Other Vehicles."

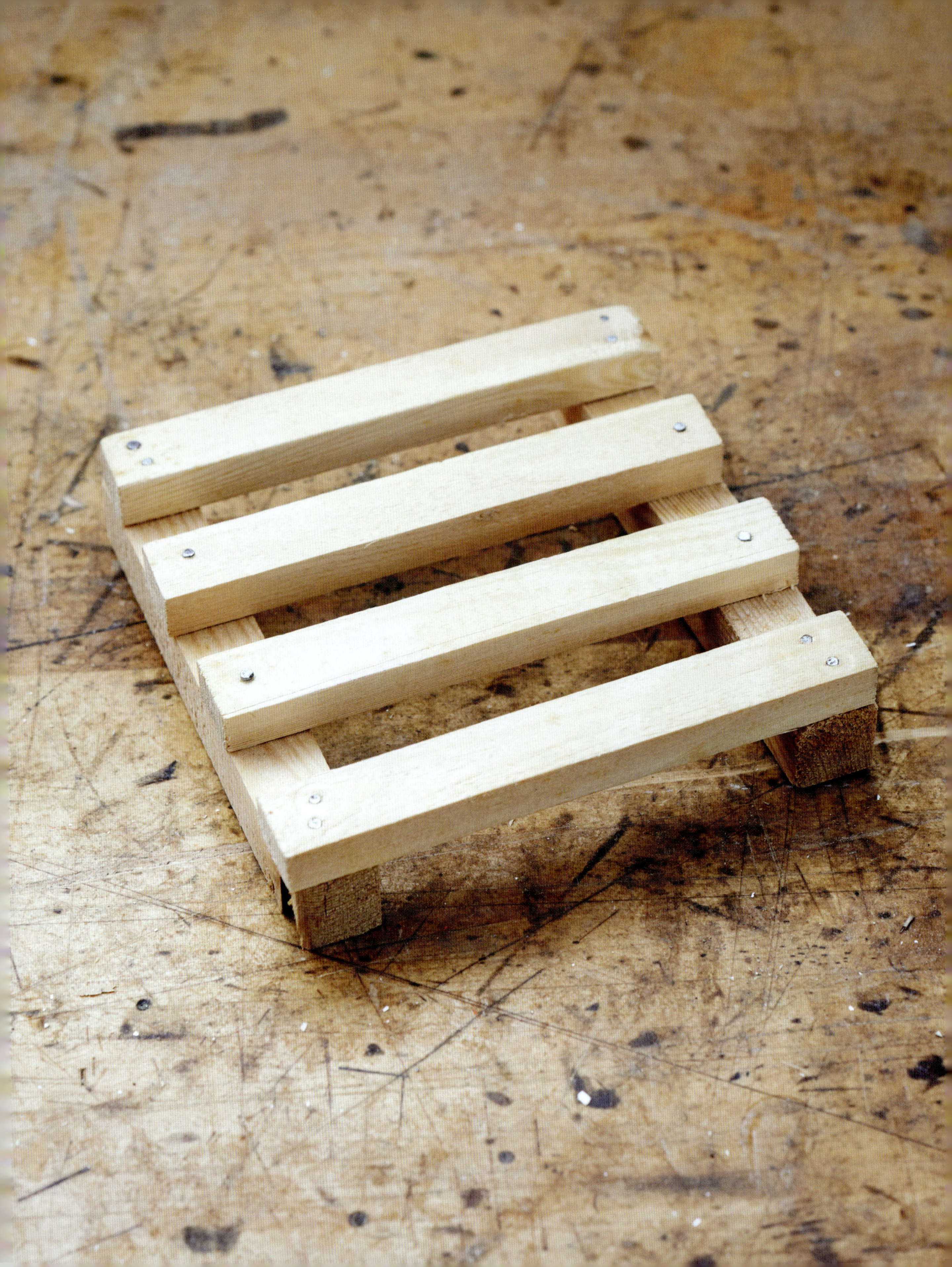

SLOYD TRIVET

In the very early days of manual-arts training and public education, children were often needed at home and on the farm to perform labor essential to their families. To send a child to school required sacrifice, so in Educational Sloyd emphasis was placed on making useful things that would serve families and build a positive relationship between home and school. A simple trivet made with strips of wood was one of the projects presented by Gustaf Larsson in Elementary Sloyd and Whittling *(Silver, Burdett & Co., 1906), which offered projects for the elementary grades. At the Clear Spring School, making these simple trivets is almost an annual project in honor of a system of manual-arts training that recognized the training of the mind and the training of the hands went hand in hand.*

MATERIALS & TOOLS

- Softwood supports, 5/8 in. thick x 3/4 in. wide x 5 1/4 in. long
- Softwood slats, 3/8 in. thick x 3/4 in. wide x 5 1/4 in. long
- 3/4 in. 18-gauge nails
- Glue
- Saw
- Hammer
- Nail set

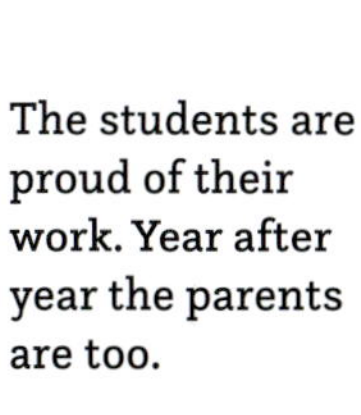

The students are proud of their work. Year after year the parents are too.

INSTRUCTIONS

1 Prepare the parts. Cut workpieces to length using a simple cutting board with a fence to align the stock. Here, a student uses a Japanese-style pull saw.

2 Sand components. A student carefully sands the surfaces and edges of the workpieces prior to beginning assembly.

3 Assemble the trivet. Use a dab of glue and 18-gauge nails ¾ in. long to secure the joints. Special care is required to align the parts to avoid shifting. Assembly with nails requires attention and it is surprising how many children these days have no experience in the use of a hammer.

A simple project that has stood the test of time helps develop woodshop skills, and results in a useful item for around the home.

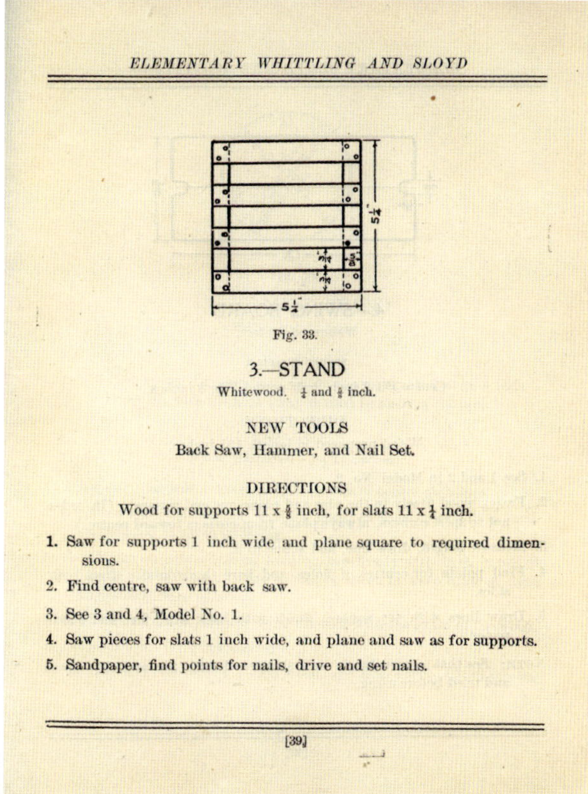

ELEMENTARY WHITTLING AND SLOYD

Fig. 33.

3.—STAND

Whitewood. ¼ and ⅜ inch.

NEW TOOLS

Back Saw, Hammer, and Nail Set.

DIRECTIONS

Wood for supports 11 x ⅜ inch, for slats 11 x ¼ inch.

1. Saw for supports 1 inch wide and plane square to required dimensions.
2. Find centre, saw with back saw.
3. See 3 and 4, Model No. 1.
4. Saw pieces for slats 1 inch wide, and plane and saw as for supports.
5. Sandpaper, find points for nails, drive and set nails.

[39]

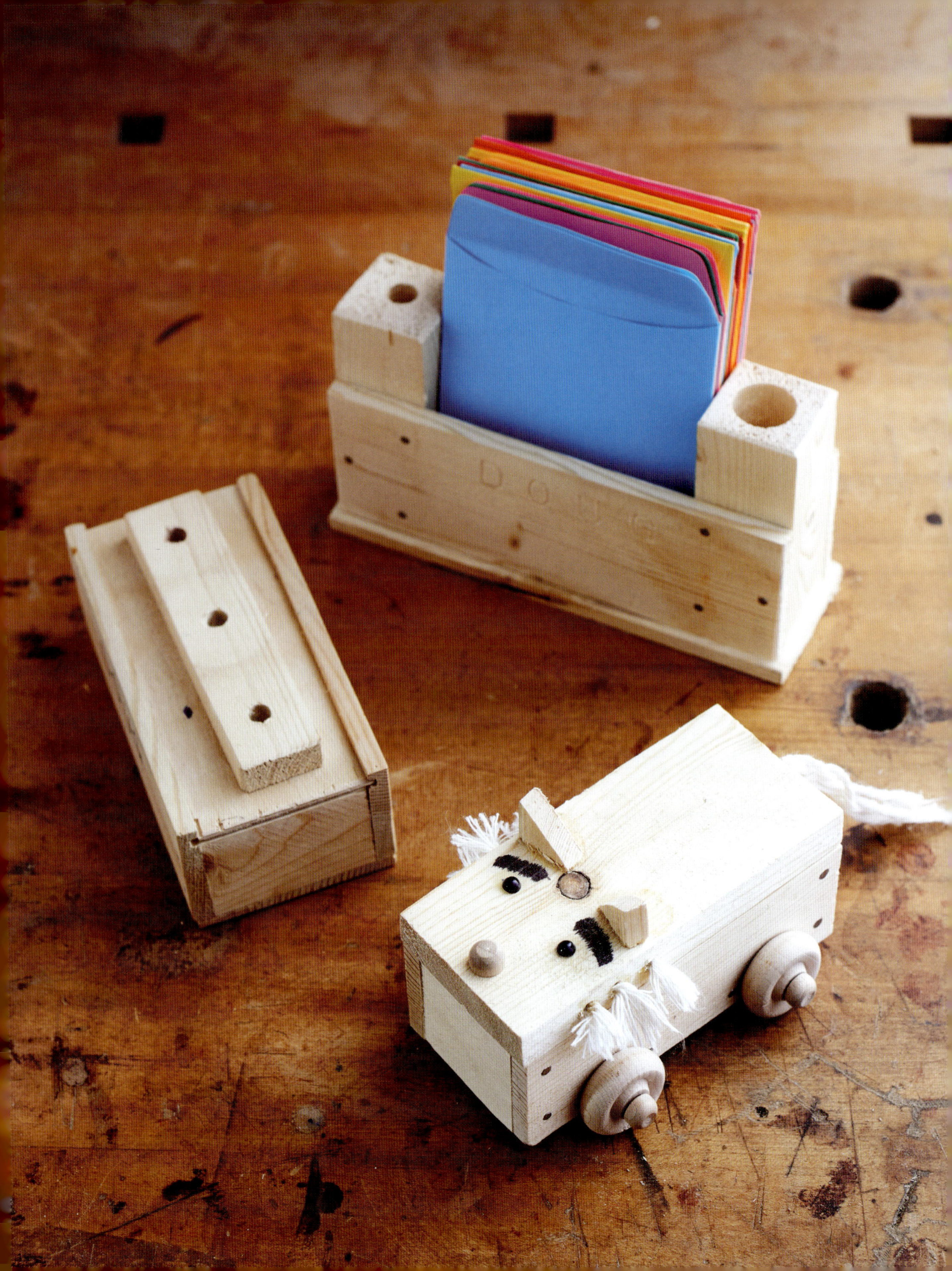

BOXES OF ALL KINDS

Box making is a favorite activity at the Clear Spring School, and at various grade levels over the years the students and I have made a wide range of designs. While many woodworking projects can be completed with little regard to accuracy, this often isn't the case for box making. In fact, there are several important skills specifically required to successfully make a box.

The first skill is that without square cuts, parts won't fit together squarely, the box won't sit well on a flat surface, and it's difficult to align corners. The box lacks strength and simply won't last.

A second skill is cutting parts to equal length or size. If one side is longer or shorter than on the other side, the box won't be square. It'll be difficult to assemble and, again, won't last.

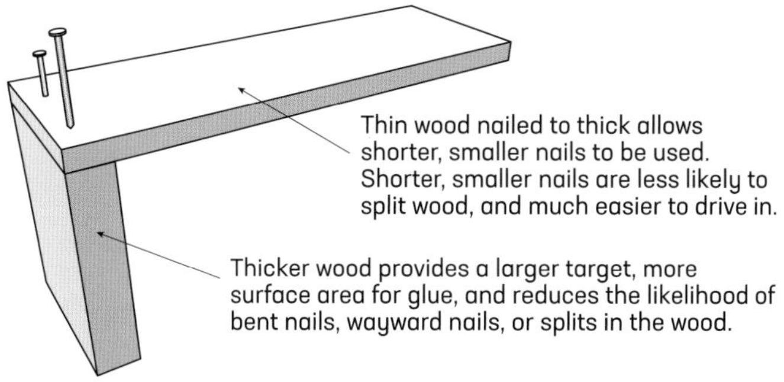

Thin wood nailed to thick allows shorter, smaller nails to be used. Shorter, smaller nails are less likely to split wood, and much easier to drive in.

Thicker wood provides a larger target, more surface area for glue, and reduces the likelihood of bent nails, wayward nails, or splits in the wood.

Nailing thin stock to thick stock gives a greater target for small nails to pass though without showing up outside the joint.

A third skill involves successful assembly. This requires attention to the alignment of parts, and holding them for gluing and nailing. This is particularly true when a box needs a lid—lids don't fit or operate well on a misshapen box.

I usually build boxes with materials of different thicknesses. Thin wood is perfect for small nails, and thicker wood provides a larger target, allowing you to assemble without nails going off course into the inside or outside of the box.

Smaller-gauge nails pass more easily through thin wood without splitting, and have sufficient length for attachment. The long nails required to pass through thicker stock, being larger in diameter, are prone to splitting wood. Thick wood being the recipient of the tip of the nail provides a wider target for the student to hit. To illustrate these three skills, I make a simple box, just as you will do in preparing a model for class.

Open boxes

The easiest boxes to make are those that are always open at the top—no lids needed!

MATERIALS & TOOLS

- 1-¼ in. square softwood
- ¼ in. thick softwood
- Nails
- Glue
- Miter box
- Saw
- Drill press with ⅜ in. and ⅝ in. drill bits
- Letter stamps

INSTRUCTIONS

A beginning-of-the-year project at the Clear Spring School is for students to make desk organizers that give them a place for pencil and scissors, and serve as a nameplate at their desks. Open on the top, this box is designed to hold 3½ in. x 5 in. colored envelopes for organizing 3x5 index cards useful to keep project information, or math facts and spelling words.

1 Prepare box components. Measure and cut the box ends first from the 1¼ in. square stock, then measure and cut the box's front and back. I use the same stock as used for the front and back to make the bottom of the box, but cut it ¼ in. longer to provide a slight overlap at the base.

2 Drill holder holes. Use a drill press to create the holes in the tops of the box ends for a pencil and scissors to fit. If working with a large group of students, you may want to prepare the ends for the boxes in advance, due to the length of time drilling can take. With a small group, let them drill the holes while you hold the workpieces. Before assembly of the box, encourage the students to sand the various parts, making the edges and surfaces smooth to the touch.

3 Do some personalization. Before nailing the front of the box in place, use letter stamps and a hammer to put the student's name on the front. You get better results in this operation before the box front is nailed in place. As an alternative, students can simply write their names on the front after the boxes are assembled.

4 **Assemble the box.** In nailing the box together, apply glue first and then position the nails to avoid the holes drilled in the end blocks. Nail the front of the box in place as shown, followed by the back. Then nail the bottom on. At this point, the students can personalize their desk sets with paint or markers.

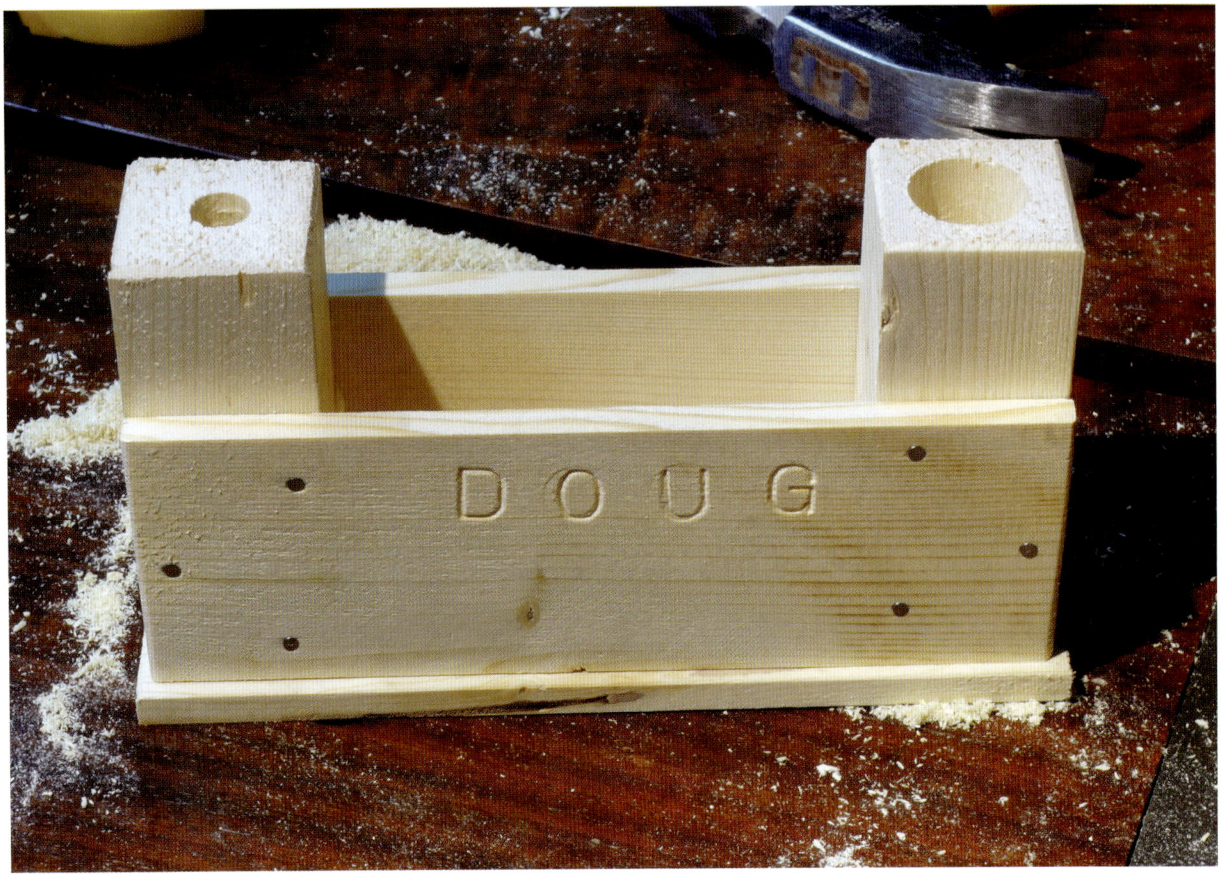

Lidded boxes

Lidded boxes offer the advantage of storing things that don't stay well or securely in an open box. They also offer a "What's inside?" sense of mystery that children love.

MATERIALS & TOOLS

- ½ in. thick softwood
- ¼ in. thick softwood
- Glue
- Nails
- Wheel axle
- Leather strips
- Tacks
- Miter box
- Hammer
- Compass
- Drill or drill press with 7/32 in. drill bit

INSTRUCTIONS

Surface-mounted metal hinges are a basic means of securing a lid to a box. However, with the younger students the tiny screws are difficult to handle, while aligning hinges accurately is challenging. At the Clear Spring School, we use other means to secure the lid to a box. Here are two options, both based on the same box.

1 **Cut the workpieces.** Use a miter box to cut the components for the main box. Here, I've stacked up several pieces of stock—front, back, lid and bottom—to cut them all to equal length at the same time.

2 **Assembly one corner first.** Get your nails started in the box sides first, and then begin assembly by securing one end piece in a vise as you align the parts. I usually put a bit of glue between parts before nailing. When you're certain the parts are in perfect alignment, drive the nails in all the way.

3 Attach the opposite end. Hold the assembled corner firmly on the bench as you nail the other end into place. Again, a bit of glue and careful alignment comes first, then nail.

4 Attach the bottom. Nail the bottom into place. I spread glue first and then drive the nails into the thicker end parts. The main box is now complete, and ready to be topped with a lid. We'll use this same box base design for both the lid methods that follow.

5 Swivel-lid box. To make a swivel-lid box, use a ½ in. thick piece of wood cut to the same size as the outside dimensions of the box. Take a compass and from a point about 5⁄16 in. from the end of the lid, swing an arc, marked in pencil about ⅔ of the way down the lid. Your kids may need some guidance on this step.

6 Separate the lid into two pieces. Mount the lid in the vise and use a coping saw to cut along the line. Try to stay exactly on the line and keep the saw blade square to the stock.

7 Begin the lid attachment. Sand the two pieces, and align the smaller piece at one end atop the box base, with the cut arc toward the center of the box. Then glue and nail the piece into place as shown.

8 Create the pivot point. To attach the swivel portion of the lid, use a drill press and 7/32 in. drill to drill the hole for the pivot pin. Align and hold the lid atop the box, then drill exactly where the point of the compass was when you scribed the arc. (The compass should have left a small hole at that spot.)

9 Glue the pivot pin in place. The pivot pin is the same 7/32 in. ready-made axle we used for car wheels earlier in the book. Before gluing the axle into place, be sure there's a small space between the two parts of the lid to allow clearance for rotation. If not, sand the curved edge to create a larger gap before attaching it.

10 Leather-hinged box. This version uses the same box base as above, but you'll need to start attaching leather hinges before the box is fully assembled, as part of the hinge must be nailed on the inside of the box. The leather hinge consists of three parts. One wide strip mounts to the inside top edge of the box, and then wraps onto the outside of the lid. Two narrower strips attach to the underside of the lid. Begin by attaching the wide a leather strip to the inside/top of the box back with tacks.

11 Attach the lid strips. Use tacks to secure the two narrow leather strips to the underside of the lid, making sure to allow enough room for the wider strip to fit between them.

12 Create the hinging action. While holding the lid in place on the top of the box, wrap the two leather strips from the underside of the lid onto the back of the box and use tacks to secure it in place. Now, wrap the leather from the inside of the box back onto the back and top of the lid. Place the tacks evenly to form a decorative pattern.

Make a Box-Car

This box is a fun one for kids to make. Simply build a pivot-lid box, but make the bottom out of ½ in. stock that will be thick enough for axle holes to be drilled. Also, make the ends thick enough for an axle pin to be used for the pivot lid. What is it? What's it to become? Use your imagination. Invite the students to use theirs. Present a model. Assign this project to a class and see what ideas they come up with on their own!

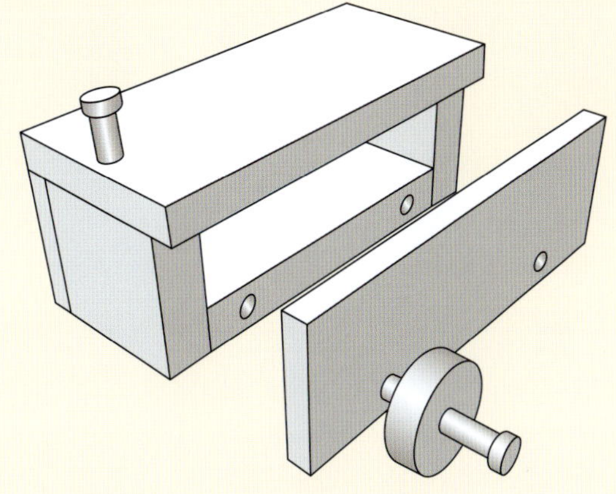

A box and car can be combined to make a box-car. Add whiskers, a nose, ears, and tail and it can be even more.

Sliding-lid box

A third option for mounting a lid without using surface-mounted metal hinges is to use a sliding lid of ⅛ in. thick Baltic birch plywood. All one needs to do to make it work is to cut grooves into the sides of the box. The box shown here was intended to hold and display toy tops.

MATERIALS & TOOLS

- ⅛ in. plywood
- ⅜ in. thick softwood
- ½ in. thick softwood
- Glue
- Nails
- Table saw
- Miter box
- Hammer

INSTRUCTIONS

1 **Time to get groovy.** Cut the 3⁄8 in. thick materials for the box sides to your desired width first, and then use the table saw to make a 1⁄8 in. x 1⁄8 in. groove 1⁄4 in. from one edge. Cut the 1⁄2 in. thick box ends 3⁄8 in. lower than the box sides to lower to provide clearance for the lid to slide over them.

2 **Size the workpieces.** Use a miter box to cut the box sides and ends to the desired length, and lightly sand.

3 **Assemble the box.** Start nails in the box sides and then secure one box end in a vise, taking care not to place nails in the inner groove. Apply a bit of glue and nail the side in place on the end piece, then remove from the vise and attach the other end in the same way. Flip the assembly over, and attach the opposite side. Then use glue and nails to assemble the box.

4 **Bottoms up.** Cut a piece of 1⁄8 in. plywood sized to the bottom of the box, and then use nails and glue to attach it. Finally, measure the distance between the bottoms of the grooves on each side, and cut a 1⁄8 in. lid to fit and slide it into place. If the lid is too tight, sand the edges for a smooth fit.

MAKING PENS

While most U.S. schools abandoning cursive writing and penmanship, at Clear Spring School we still practice with pens dipped in ink. For extra fun, the pens are ones the kids have made themselves, either turned on the lathe or carved with a knife. So writing is greeted with enthusiasm, even at the high school level.

A selection of whittled and lathe-turned pens in a variety of wood species.

The crucial part at the start is to drill a hole in the pen blank for the nib to fit. I have for many years used a simple device I made for the drill press to hold the pen blank in a precise vertical position under the drill. It takes a few test holes in stock to adjust it so the drill goes right into the center of the pen blank, and it must be adjusted to the proper depth so that the nib doesn't push in too deeply.

To make the pen-holding stand for the drill press, take two pieces of particleboard and join them at the end in a right angle. Apply an angle piece as shown to stiffen the assembly and add a vertical fence to position the pen blank.

Another option is a commercially available jig. This pen-drilling jig is centered over the hole in the table of the drill press to provide clearance for the pen blank to extend below the table directly under the tip of the drill. I added

A simple device for holding a pen blank vertically on the drill press allows drilling a precisely centered hole at a precise depth to hold the nib.

Drilling with a pen-turner's vise gaurantees precision. (They're also useful for drilling wheels.)

the board underneath the jig to make clamping to the drill press table easier.

Again, center the jig under the drill bit and adjust the depth stop so the drill goes no deeper than required for the nib to fit.

With both jigs, I use a 7⁄32 in. drill bit to fit the nibs that I purchased online. For both types of pen, either turned or whittled, a small dowel is required in the hole to steady the nib.

The nib and a 3⁄16 in. dowel fit into the hole drilled in the end of the pen blank. In some cases a bit of glue is also required for a tighter fit.

WORKING WITH THE LATHE

For lathe-turned pens, I add a block of wood to the faceplate and drill a hole exactly at center. The hole should be the size of the square pen blank you've prepared. Use a chisel to square the round hole so that the pen blank will fit. This will be mounted on the drive (headstock) side of the lathe. The end of the pen blank with the nib hole fits neatly into a standard free-spinning tailstock.

Use a small gouge to round the square pen blank and then use your lathe skills and design sense to turn a pen shape pleasing to you. When you get a shape you like, use sandpaper to smooth your work. Apply finish while it is still on the

A specially crafted faceplate holds the pen blank on the lathe.

Use a free-spinning tail center to hold the pen blank at the other end.

A light touch with a small gouge quickly rounds the pen stock. When you've created a slender cylinder, add detail.

lathe and polish it smooth. For this pen I used quick-drying shellac. Then use a gouge, a skew, or a parting tool to cut through at the drive end of the lathe, freeing the completed pen from the lathe.

Whittling pens is easier to do using the whittling techniques described in "The Knife" Chapter in the tool section earlier in this book. This work can begin as early as first grade, preparing a student to feel even better prepared to learn to write.

Sand the pen while it is spinning on the lathe.

Use a lathe chisel to cut the blank from the chuck. Remove the small stub that remains in the face-plate with pliers.

Whittling a pen is a perfect introduction for the younger children. Use the tools, techniques and safety hints beginning on page 13.

FURNITURE

Furniture is one of the areas of woodworking that interests students of all ages at the Clear Spring School. Even in first grade, students attempt to make small tables and chairs by adding dowels to the underside of pieces of plywood using nails and glue.

The fact that these experiments may fail or disappoint would be of no surprise to an adult, but hands-on experimentation is one of the best ways to learn. Observing the cause of failure may be just as meaningful as achieving success. I rarely interject my own opinions about what will or will not work unless I'm asked, as the experimentation is as of much value as success.

A drill-based tenoner and matching drill bit can be used to create beautiful and lasting furniture, and allow for student experimentation in furniture design.

Our emphasis is on learning design and engineering, rather than simply making things according to a prescribed plan, as this allows students of all ages to test their own ideas hands-on.

Some of our best high school work has involved simple techniques using a drill-powered tenoner to form round tenons on the ends of a pieces of wood. The tenons fit into holes drilled into an adjoining piece of wood, forming what is called a mortise-and-tenon joint, one of the key building blocks of traditional furniture making. These joints are round, making them very easy to create. With the exception of the tenoner itself, no real specialized equipment is required. In fact, an entire furniture program can be built with this tool serving as its core. Other tools can be added for more complex or refined work.

Using the tenoner, the student simply clamps a piece of wood in the vise and, holding the tool and drill level, forms the

With wood held in the vise and the tenoner locked in the drill chuck, a student carefully guides the drill to form the round tenon.

tenon. The tenoner mounted in a drill works like a very large pencil sharpener. The wood can either be in the form of branches cut from tree trimming or hardwood squares or octagonal stock. Using the same drill with a drill bit matched in size to the tenoner forms the mortise into which the tenon fits. We usually drill the hole all the way through the stock so that the tenon can be wedged from the other side to tighten it in place.

For rustic furniture work, simple hand tools are perfectly acceptable, as well as low-cost materials that challenge the student, but would likely be overlooked by some craftsmen.

This work is an excellent introduction to what Harvard educators have called "Studio Thinking." And yet the results can be as refined as the student's temperament and interests allow, resulting in heirloom work.

For rustic work, a handsaw will suffice, as the saw marks can add to the overall charm and character of the piece. The effort has its own rewards.

Fitting odd pieces to formulate something from the mind's eye is an exercise in design and engineering. "Studio Thinking."

Student work can be refined with a few additional woodworking tools to become of heirloom quality.

Student work with rustic materials or more conventional dimensioned woods is sometimes wildly creative and involves intricate engineering.

RESOURCES

METRIC CONVERSIONS

In this book, lengths are given in inches. If you want to convert those to metric measurements, please use the following formulas:

Fractions to Decimals

⅛ = .125

¼ = .25

½ = .5

⅝ = .625

¾ = .75

Imperial to Metric Conversion

Multiply inches by 25.4 to get millimeters

Multiply inches by 2.54 to get centimeters

Multiply yards by .9144 to get meters

For example, if you wanted to convert 1⅛ inches to millimeters:

1.125 in. x 25.4mm = 28.575mm

And to convert 2½ yards to meters:

2.5 yd. x .9144m = 2.286m

CONVERSIONS

Fractions to Decimal Equivalents (Inches)

1/64	.015625	33/64	.515625
1/32	.031250	17/32	.531250
3/64	.046875	35/64	.546875
1/16	.062500	9/16	.562500
5/64	.078125	37/64	.578125
3/32	.093750	19/32	.593750
7/64	.109375	39/64	.609375
1/8	.125000	5/8	.625000
9/64	.140625	41/64	.640625
5/32	.156250	21/32	.656250
11/64	.171875	43/64	.671875
3/16	.187500	11/16	.687500
13/64	.203125	45/64	.703125
7/32	.218750	23/32	.718750
15/64	.234375	47/64	.734375
1/4	.250000	3/4	.750000
17/64	.265625	49/64	.765625
9/32	.281250	25/32	.781250
19/64	.296875	51/64	.796875
5/16	.312500	13/16	.812500
21/64	.328125	53/64	.828125
11/32	.343750	27/32	.843750
23/64	.359375	55/64	.859375
3/8	.375000	7/8	.875000
25/64	.390625	57/64	.890625
13/32	.406250	29/32	.906250
27/64	.421875	59/64	.921875
7/16	.437500	15/16	.937500
29/64	.453125	61/64	.953125
15/32	.468750	31/32	.968750
31/64	.484375	63/64	.984375
1/2	.500000	1	1.00000

Inches to Millimeters (Fractions to Decimal Equivalents)

1/64	0.396875	33/64	13.09688
1/32	0.793750	17/32	13.49375
3/64	1.190625	35/64	13.89063
1/16	1.587500	9/16	14.28750
5/64	1.984375	37/64	14.68438
3/32	2.381250	19/32	15.08125
7/64	2.778125	39/64	15.47813
1/8	3.175000	5/8	15.87500
9/64	3.571875	41/64	16.27188
5/32	3.968750	21/32	16.66875
11/64	4.365625	43/64	17.06563
3/16	4.762500	11/16	17.46250
13/64	5.159375	45/64	17.85938
7/32	5.556250	23/32	18.25625
15/64	5.953125	47/64	18.65313
1/4	6.350000	3/4	19.05000
17/64	6.746875	49/64	19.44688
9/32	7.143750	25/32	19.84375
19/64	7.540625	51/64	20.24063
5/16	7.937500	13/16	20.63750
21/64	8.334375	53/64	21.03438
11/32	8.731250	27/32	21.43125
23/64	9.128125	55/64	21.82813
3/8	9.525000	7/8	22.22500
25/64	9.921875	57/64	22.62188
13/32	10.31875	29/32	23.01875
27/64	10.71563	59/64	23.41563
7/16	11.11250	15/16	23.81250
29/64	11.50938	61/64	24.20938
15/32	11.90625	31/32	24.60625
31/64	12.30313	63/64	25.00313
1/2	12.70000	1	25.40000

ABOUT THE AUTHOR

Doug Stowe has been a professional woodworker in Eureka Springs, Arkansas, since 1976. He began writing books and articles about woodworking in 1994. He started teaching woodworking to adults about that time, and, with the help of the Windgate Foundation went on to teach children at the Clear Spring School in 2001. In 2009, he was named an Arkansas Living Treasure for his contributions to the practice and furtherance of traditional crafts.

"We learn best and to greatest lasting effect when we learn hands-on and by doing real things. Through woodworking, children can be of service to family, community, and self and gain in intelligence and character by doing so."

Doug Stowe

ACKNOWLEDGMENTS

I want to thank the children, parents, teachers, administration, and board of the Clear Spring School, without whom this book would not have been possible. I'm grateful for the Windgate Foundation for their support for the arts, and in particular for their support of my Wisdom of the Hands program at the Clear Spring School. When we launched this program in 2001, school woodshops were disappearing at an alarming rate and were widely thought to be a thing of the past. We've provided strong evidence that all children can benefit from woodworking, regardless of their educational or career ambitions. And just as I learned many years ago, our brains are in our hands.

I also want to thank Matthew Teague, editor A.J. Hamler, designers Lindsay Hess and Alicia Freile, and the entire team at Blue Hills Press.

INDEX

Note: Page numbers in *italics* indicate projects.

MORE GREAT BOOKS *from*
BLUE HILLS PRESS

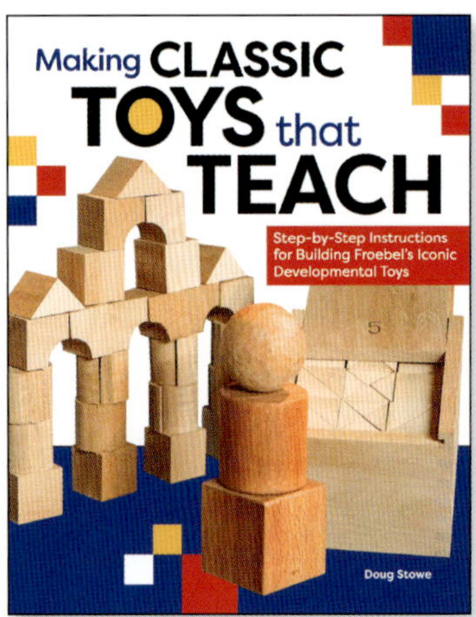

Making Classic Toys that Teach
$29.95 | 144 Pages

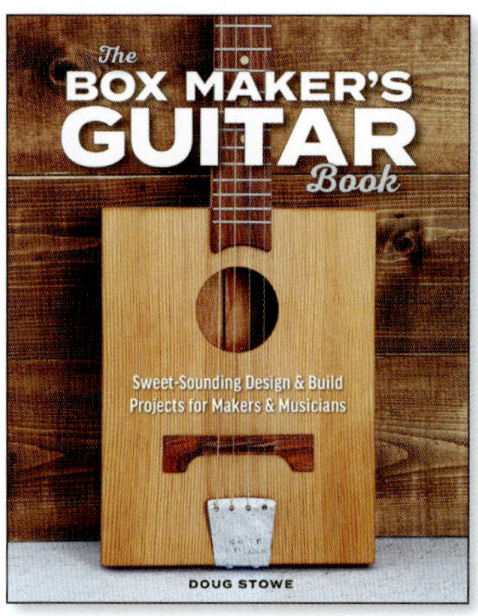

The Box Maker's Guitar Book
$27.95 | 168 Pages

Essential Joinery
$29.95 | 216 Pages

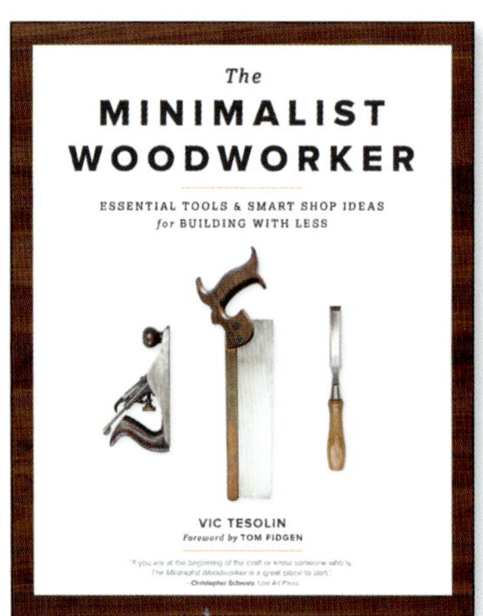

The Minimalist Woodworker
$27.95 | 152 Pages

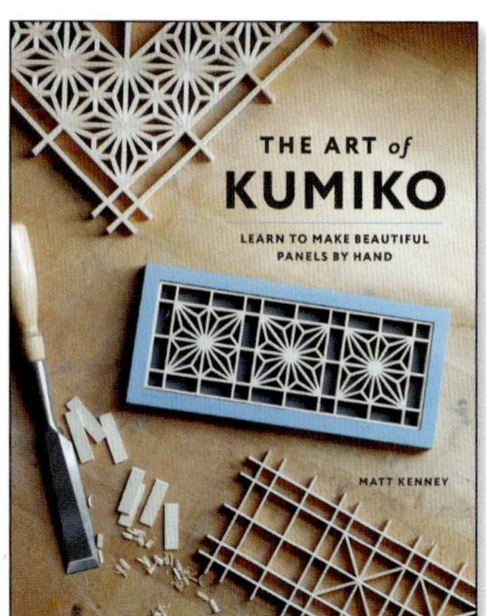

The Art of Kumiko
$27.95 | 168 Pages

Look for these Blue Hills Press titles at your favorite bookstore, specialty retailer, or visit *www.bluehillspress.com*.
For more information about Blue Hills Press, email us at *info@bluehillspress.com*.